A *Perfect* MATCH

A Guide to Precise Machine Piecing

Revised and Updated With All New Quilts

Donna Lynn Thomas

DEDICATION

This book is dedicated to my mother, Mary Louise Smith Brooks, who not only gave me the gift of life, but also the skill and passion for sewing to help see me through that life. More than that, she has loved me through thick and thin and at times when I haven't deserved it. She's always there for me even when we're continents apart. I love you dearly, Mother!

ACKNOWLEDGMENTS

As always, there are a lot of wonderful people who help with the birth of a book. These people all deserve special accolades for their hard work. A hearty thanks to all!

To Ann Woodward, Dee Glenn, Robin Chambers, Deb Rose, and Kari Lane for their pattern testing and quiltmaking expertise;

To Judy Keller and Kari Lane for their beautiful quilting that breathes life into any quilt;

To my friend Ursula Reikes who always has time for a "quick" phone call;

To the staff at That Patchwork Place and my editor, Sally Schneider, for doing such a wonderful job.

Thanks to each of you from the bottom of my heart!

MISSION STATEMENT

We are dedicated to providing quality products and service by working together to inspire creativity and to enrich the lives we touch.

CREDITS

Editor-in-Chief .... Kerry I. Smith
Technical Editors .... Sally Schneider
Ursula Reikes
Managing Editor .... Judy Petry
Design Director, Cover Designer .... Cheryl Stevenson
Text Designer .... Kay Green
Production Assistant .... Marijane E. Figg
Copy Editor .... Liz McGehee
Proofreader .... Tina Cook
Illustrator .... Laurel Strand
Photographer .... Brent Kane

A Perfect Match: A Guide to Precise Machine Piecing
© 1998 by Donna Lynn Thomas

Martingale & Company
PO Box 118
Bothell, WA 98041-0118 USA

Printed in the United States of America
02 01 00 99 98 97   6 5 4 3 2 1

Library of Congress Cataloging-in-Publication Data
Thomas, Donna Lynn,
    A perfect match : a guide to precise machine piecing /
Donna Lynn Thomas — Rev. and updated.
        p. cm.
    ISBN 1-56477-153-9
    1. Machine quilting—Patterns. 2. Patchwork—Patterns.
I. Title.
TT835T43 1998
746.46—dc21   97-31533
                                                   CIP

Table of Contents

Introduction

I was first introduced to a needle at the tender age of four. My mother was a home-economics teacher, and she started me out on a pretty little cross-stitch heart project (that I still have—unfinished!). Her special interest was tailoring and garment construction. I remember many a night falling asleep to the whir of her machine as she worked on her latest project. I guess it was natural that not too many years later, my sisters and I were personally introduced to her sewing machine and the wonders of fabric. My mother has never made a quilt, and I stopped making clothes many years ago when I discovered quilts, but neither of us can imagine life without a sewing machine.

Whether by machine or by hand, a quilt must be stitched. *A Perfect Match* is about machine piecing, whether the pieces are marked with templates and a sewing line or rotary cut with seam allowances included. Along with stitching basics, you will find information on stitching many types of special seams, no matter how you mark or cut your pieces. I have included a quick review of marking and cutting techniques to get you off to a good start.

I have also included all the tips, techniques, and tidbits of knowledge I have acquired over the years from many people, beginning with my mother. I learned many other things through hours of quiet frustration, struggling alone with each new quilting challenge.

Six quilt plans are presented in *A Perfect Match*. They provide you with the opportunity to practice the stitching techniques covered in the book. Five are presented in both template and rotary-cut versions, so you may choose the method you prefer; the sixth is written only for template construction.

Machine piecing can be extremely rewarding, not only because of its speed but also because of the extreme accuracy you can achieve. Master these skills, and all your quilts will be a "perfect match!"

About the Author

Donna has been quilting since 1975 and teaching since 1982. The introduction of rotary-cutting tools in the early 1980s revolutionized her approach to quiltmaking. Since Nancy Martin introduced her to bias strip piecing in 1987, Donna has worked extensively with this technique, developing new uses and innovative ways to maximize precision piecing.

In 1995, Donna presented her new tool, the Bias Stripper, in conjunction with her new bias strip-piecing concepts. She continues to explore different ways to use the tool for other techniques.

Donna is the author of five other books: *Small Talk, Shortcuts: A Concise Guide to Rotary Cutting, Shortcuts to the Top, Stripples,* and *Stripples Strikes Again!*

Equipment and Supplies

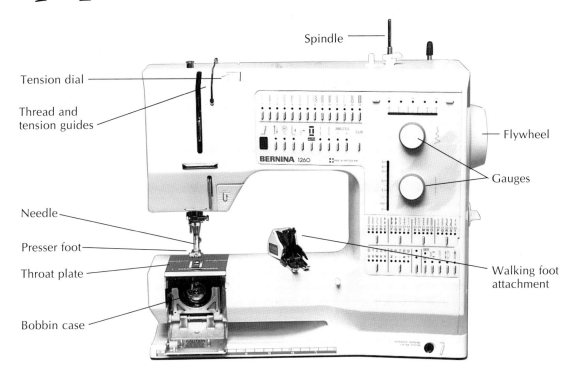

Spindle

Tension dial

Thread and tension guides

Flywheel

Gauges

Needle

Presser foot

Throat plate

Walking foot attachment

Bobbin case

BERNINA 1260

THE SEWING MACHINE

The most important piece of equipment for machine piecing is your sewing machine. It does not need to be fancy; all that's necessary is a machine that stitches forward and backward with a fine-quality straight stitch. Like any piece of equipment, it should be properly maintained, and you should be familiar with its parts and operation. Take the time to read your owner's manual if you haven't already—you'll be surprised what you can learn from it.

In addition to a yearly professional service, clean and oil your machine regularly, following the directions in the manual. Generally, this involves a simple cleaning under the throat plate and in the bobbin housing to remove lint buildup. Oiling methods vary from machine to machine, so check your manual. If you clean the machine every time you begin a new quilt, you and your machine should spend many happy years together. Your local dealer can answer any specific questions you may have concerning your machine, its care, and operation. If he can't help, write the manufacturer.

The basic parts of a sewing machine are shown above. Many newer machines have considerably more features, but those listed are the most important.

SPINDLE. This is the projection at the top right that holds the spool of thread so it feeds evenly through the thread guides.

THREAD AND TENSION GUIDES. There are usually several types of these that the thread winds around or passes through on its way to the needle. Every manufacturer has its own system of guides, so take the time to study your manual or consult your local dealer for the proper way to thread your particular machine. The combined function of the various thread guides is to control the tension and feeding of the thread to the needle for fine, even stitching. If the thread snaps or the stitching quality is poor or loose, the problem is often improper threading of the machine. Always check the guides first when you encounter stitching problems.

TENSION DIAL. This dial is located on the front of the machine and can be used to adjust the tension of the upper thread. There is a standard setting for this tension. The standard setting is usually correct for quilt-weight fabric, and adjustments are normally made for specialty fabrics, such as silk or denim, and threads, such as metallic or rayon machine-embroidery thread.

BOBBIN AND BOBBIN CASE. The bobbin is the small metal spool that is wound with thread; it is loaded under the sewing platform to make the bottom half of the stitch. The bobbin not only supplies the bottom thread but also controls the tension of that thread. If thread is bunching up on the underside of your seams or the bottom thread tension is loose, check to make sure the bobbin is wound and loaded properly. If you are not sure, consult your manual or dealer for the proper way to load the bobbin. Most machines require professional servicing to adjust the bobbin tension.

NEEDLE. There are various types of needles available for machine stitching. The preferred needle for quiltmaking is a standard, fine, Sharp needle, size 80/12. Ball-point needles are inappropriate for cottons. The rounded tip on a ball-point needle is designed to slide between rather than pierce the threads of synthetic fabrics to prevent snagging. All machine needles become dull with continued use and should be changed frequently. A good rule of thumb is to change your needle when you start a new quilt. You can tell your needle is dull if you hear a "popping" sound every time the needle pierces the fabric. If you sew over pins, your needle will dull or break more frequently, and this can affect the quality of your stitching.

PRESSER FOOT. The standard utility presser foot that comes with your machine is all you need for machine piecing. It is generally broad and flat, sometimes with a gap in the front bar, directly in front of the needle, so you can see where you are stitching. Most people assume the outer right-hand edge of the presser foot is ¼" from the needle and use it as their seam guide, but this is not always the case. See "Stitching an Accurate Seam Allowance" on page 18.

THROAT PLATE. This is the metal plate under the needle. It has an oval hole on machines with zigzag capabilities and a circular hole on machines that sew only straight stitches. A special straight-stitch throat plate can usually be purchased to replace the one with the zigzag opening. This is helpful for machines that tend to "eat" fabric through the wider zigzag opening. Most throat plates have standard seam allowances marked to the right of the needle. Periodically, remove the throat plate to clean the area around the feed dogs, removing the lint, dust, and soil that collect there.

FEED DOGS. The feed dogs consist of the bar with teethlike moving pieces that project through the slots in the throat plate. These teeth move from front to back and up and down in a circular motion to grasp the fabric, provide bottom pressure as it is being stitched, and then move the fabric away from the needle toward the back of the machine. Because of this grasp-and-release action, the feed dogs help ease in any excess fullness in the lower layer of fabric in a seam. The standard presser foot, on the other hand, provides constant pressure on the upper layer and sometimes pushes the top layer of fabric forward in front of the needle.

WALKING FOOT. This special presser foot is not essential, but it is helpful when you are stitching through thick layers, quilting by machine, or handling excess fullness in one of the seam layers. In addition to being attached to the shank that holds the presser foot, it is also attached to the arm that holds the needle. This causes the walking foot to move up and down in conjunction with the movement of the needle, providing pressure on the fabric when the needle is down and releasing pressure when the needle is up. The walking foot "walks" over the fabric rather than pushes it along like the standard foot. Combined with the grasp-and-release action of the feed dogs, the walking foot is an excellent tool for machine quilting, since both layers are fed at the same speed.

Note: Some sewing machines have a built-in, even-feed feature that accomplishes the same thing as the walking foot.

FLYWHEEL. The large, round wheel on the right side of the machine can be turned to move the needle up and down. There are times when you want to do a few manual stitches; some machines also need a few manual turns of the wheel to help with the first few power-driven stitches. Unless your machine has an automatic needle-down setting, use this wheel every time you stop stitching to end with the needle down in the fabric.

GAUGES. On the front of most machines, several gauges, switches, or dials regulate stitch length, stitch width, and sometimes needle position. Newer machines may have a host of other adjustments. Refer to your manual to make any gauge adjustments. Listed below are the standard settings for machine piecing:

Stitch width: Set for straight stitch, not zigzag.

Stitch length: 12 stitches per inch or your machine's equivalent. On European machines, use the standard setting of 2 or 2½.

Needle position: This is normally set at the center, but sometimes it is adjusted slightly to the right on zigzag machines to provide an accurate ¼"-wide seam guide (remember to use a zigzag throat plate if your needle position is off-center). Not all machines have adjustable needle positions. It's not essential, so don't worry if yours doesn't.

OTHER BASIC SUPPLIES

ROTARY EQUIPMENT. If you plan to use rotary-cutting techniques, you will need a rotary cutter, a rotary-cutting mat, and a good acrylic ruler with clear markings. Some of the rotary-cutting directions in this book require the Bias Square® ruler. Detailed use of these and other special rotary supplies is described in *Shortcuts: A Concise Guide to Rotary Cutting*.

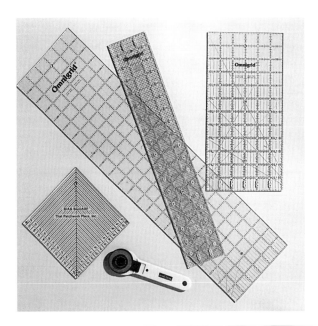

If you prefer to use templates, you will need the following items. You may also need them if you plan to adapt template-cut patterns for rotary cutting.

GRAPH PAPER, RULER, AND PENCIL. It is a good idea to check the accuracy of templates for a particular pattern before making your own. Draft the full-size block on graph paper, then check the templates against the pattern. Investigate any differences to determine whether it's your error or an incorrect pattern. Much time and fabric can be saved by taking this simple precaution. Be sure to buy fine-line drafting-quality graph paper from an office-supply store, quilt shop, or other professional source. Graph paper found in a supermarket or dime store is often inaccurate. Eight squares per inch is best, but four is adequate.

COMPASS AND PROTRACTOR. Use these to draft designs with curves and angles.

TEMPLATE MATERIAL. The best material is translucent plastic, since it is easily marked and cut and lasts longer than cardboard. You can see through it for correct positioning when you want a particular section of a print to fall in a certain spot on a piece.

UTILITY SCISSORS. Use these instead of your good fabric scissors to cut template plastic.

LEAD AND COLORED PENCILS. These should be kept sharp so you can accurately mark the fabric. A good #2 lead pencil will mark clearly on the majority of fabrics, but on some fabrics, sewing and cutting lines are more visible with a bright yellow, silver, or orange pencil. Hard, colored leads keep their points better, resulting in fine marking lines. Look for a basic set of good-quality colored pencils at most art- or office-supply stores.

FABRIC SHEARS. Good, sharp shears are a must for cutting accurate fabric pieces, although rotary equipment can also be used to cut out marked pieces.

SANDPAPER BOARD. This is an easily constructed and invaluable tool for accurately marking fabric. Glue fine sandpaper to a hard surface, such as wood, cardboard, poster board, linoleum squares, or needlework mounting board. The sticky surface on a mounting board eliminates the need for more glue—just stick the sandpaper in place! I have two sandpaper boards: one is 8" x 10", small enough to be portable, and the other is about 16" x 20" for my work at home.

PINS. Use silk pins for cotton. They are long, slender, and sharp, making it easy to pin very precisely at corners and intersections. Colored glass heads are not essential, but many quiltmakers prefer them for their visibility.

SEAM RIPPER. This item is essential, not only for "unsewing" seams, but also for use as a "better finger," as described in "Blue Ribbon Stitching Techniques" on page 23.

IRONING SUPPLIES. Good ironing supplies need not be fancy, just clean and operable. The ironing surface can be a traditional ironing board or just a simple terry-cloth towel placed on a heat-resistant surface. Use a clean, dry iron (no steam) on the cotton setting. Use distilled water in the spray barrel, especially if you have hard water. Hard water will leave mineral deposits in your iron that will not only clog the spray nozzle and ruin the iron, but may also eventually be expelled onto your fabric through the steam vents. If you do not have a spray feature on your iron, an ordinary spray bottle is a handy substitute. Do not use the same spray bottle for your fabrics that you use for any household chemicals; use it only for water.

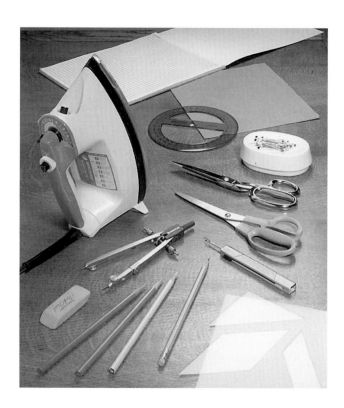

Fabric Preparation

SELECTING FABRIC

I prefer to use 100% cottons for my quilts. That is not to say that, on occasion, I haven't found a perfect print in a polyester/cotton blend. There are advantages to cottons that make it the fabric of choice for most quiltmakers. With the huge variety and consistent quality of 100% cotton fabric from the major manufacturers, not to mention the beautiful designer lines available to us now, it's easy to use them exclusively these days.

Not only has cotton passed the test of time for durability, but it has the charming ability to adhere to other cottons. Synthetics, on the other hand, are often quite slippery. Cottons are easier to handle and manage. Cottons also do not fray as easily as synthetics and they crease nicely, making it easy to get tight, clean intersections and seams. When you align or press a cotton, it is much more likely to stay put. It is a "quilter-friendly" fabric.

PREWASHING

Cottons, cotton blends, and cottons of different weights can shrink at different rates, so it is best to prewash all fabrics before combining them in a quilt. If one fabric is already prewashed, it is wise to prewash the rest too. Prewashing removes the sizing and the considerable amount of dust and dirt accumulated in the manufacturing and shipping process. Add spray sizing for extra body, if desired, when pressing the fabrics dry.

It is extremely important to pretest fabric for bleeding before washing. This simple step can prevent many a ruined quilt. There are two terms you will hear in reference to color loss in fabrics: crocking and bleeding.

Crocking is not uncommon and is the rubbing off of excess dye from the surface of the fabric. One or two washings usually removes this excess dye.

Bleeding occurs when the dye has not been properly fixed to the fabric. Continued washing does not stop the run of dye into the water. If used in a quilt, the dye will bleed into nearby fabrics, marring the quilt permanently. Vinegar and salt baths are only temporary solutions. Their effects eventually disappear, and bleeding can resume.

Test for bleeding by cutting a 6" square of each dyed fabric. Drop it into a jar of very hot water and wait twenty minutes. If the water is clear after twenty minutes, the fabric is safe. If the water changes color, test again with the same swatch to see if the water runs clear a second or third time. This will help you determine whether you need to wash the yardage more than once to remove excess dye (crocking). If the fabric continues to run after several baths, I would suspect a poorly fixed dye. I recommend discarding the fabric or trying one of the new dye fixatives, such as Retayne, now available in quilt and craft stores.

When washing fabrics and quilts, avoid detergents. With time, detergents can weaken the bond between a dye and cotton, resulting in fading and possible bleeding later. One of the simplest and safest cleansers is plain, sudsy ammonia. Not only is it inexpensive, but it rinses out completely in one rinse. Use one-quarter cup in the washing machine or a tablespoonful for the average-sized sink. When used in the proper proportions, there is no residual ammonia odor in the fabric.

Wash both fabric and finished quilts in warm, not hot or cold, water (remember, it was only squares we tested in hot water). Extremely hot or cold water is damaging to natural fibers, such as cotton or wool. I wash large quantities of fabric in the washing machine on gentle cycle and small quantities in a sink. A large number of small pieces can be machine washed easily in lingerie bags to avoid tangling and knotting.

Once washed, machine dry on low or fluff, or hang the fabric until it is damp-dry. Cotton tends to become heavily wrinkled if dried bone-dry in the dryer. Iron the fabric smooth when damp-dry and you will have wrinkle-free cotton. Your fabric is now ready to be used in your quilts.

FOLLOWING THE GRAIN LINE

There are three types of fabric grain. Yarns running parallel to the selvage are the lengthwise grain. This grain has little or no give. Yarns running perpendicular to the selvage are the crosswise grain and have a small amount of give. Template edges marked parallel to either of these grains are generally considered to be on-grain. Bias is any direction other than these two grains, although true bias runs at a 45° angle to the lengthwise or crosswise grain. The bias grain stretches and distorts very easily.

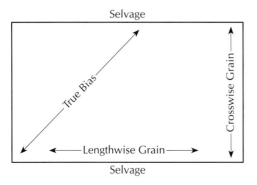

There are two rules of thumb to follow when trying to decide which edges to mark on-grain.
1. Place all edges that will be on the perimeter of a quilt block on the straight grain.
2. Whenever possible, without violating rule number one, sew a bias edge to a straight edge to stabilize the bias edge. Sometimes, both rules are thrown to the wind in favor of design or other considerations. In such a situation, bias edges can be tamed with a little spray sizing or careful stay stitching ⅛" from the raw edge.

Cutting Fabric

There are three methods for marking and cutting fabric; the first two require templates. With the first method, you mark the sewing lines; with the second, the seam allowances are included in the templates. The third method is to use rotary equipment to cut pieces with seam allowances included, eliminating the need to make templates.

USING TEMPLATES

When using templates, care and accuracy in each step of construction and use is important. Because there are several steps, small inaccuracies in each step will compound the problem.

Whether making templates with or without seam allowances, begin with an accurate drawing of the finished pattern piece. Add ¼"-wide seam allowances to all sides if you want to include the seam allowances, then transfer the pattern to plastic template material. Mark the points and/or corners of the shape on the plastic first, then use a straight edge to draw the lines in between.

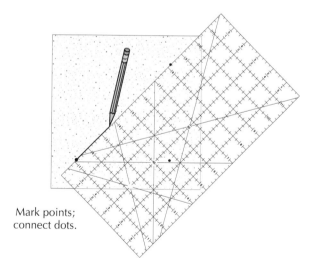

Mark points;
connect dots.

Cut templates from plastic, using sharp scissors. Cut past the corners, not around them, to keep them accurate.

Templates must be marked accurately on the fabric. Place the templates face down on the wrong side of the fabric. Work on a sandpaper board to keep the fabric from slipping. Fine sandpaper will grip the fabric so it doesn't shift, but is fine enough so the pencil doesn't wobble as you trace. Mark along the sides of the template with a sharp, hard lead or colored pencil held at an angle. The angle keeps the point sharp so it moves over the fabric smoothly. A pencil held upright can get caught between the threads in the weave of the fabric, causing it to drag and distort the line. The point wears down faster, too, causing marking inaccuracies.

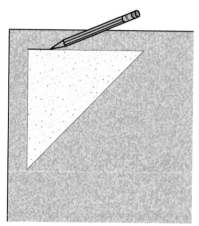

Hold pencil point at an angle.

To keep corners well defined, do not trace around the corners; instead, extend the side lines past the corners, forming accurate cross hairs.

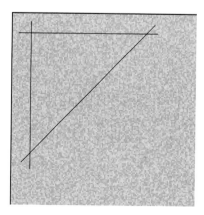

Extend lines past corners.

For templates with marked sewing lines, cut ¼" away from the line. For templates with seam allowances included, cut right on the line, not to either side. A rotary cutter can be used to cut pieces both with and without seam allowances.

When you've marked only the sewing line on the fabric, align the ¼" mark on the ruler with the drawn line to cut an accurate seam allowance around a piece.

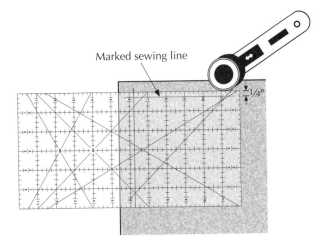

Marked sewing line

When cutting pieces with seam allowances included, align the edge of the ruler with the drawn line.

TIP

When cutting many pieces with seam allowances included, cut the fabric in layers with the rotary cutter. Cut and stack four to six layers of fabric, right sides down. Mark the top layer only and cut through all layers at once.

SIMPLE ROTARY CUTTING

There are many techniques specific to rotary cutting, but the most important tips for accuracy are simple. For more extensive, in-depth discussion of rotary techniques, please see my other books: *Shortcuts, Stripples,* and *Stripples Strikes Again!*

Most rotary cutting involves cutting strips that are then sewn into strip units or crosscut into other shapes. To cut accurate strips, you need to create an even cutting edge first.

1. Fold the fabric selvage to selvage, then press. Lay the fabric on the cutting mat with the fold toward you.
2. Place your ruler just inside the raw edges of all the fabric layers at the left edge (or right edge if you are left-handed). Place the edge or horizontal line of a second ruler on the folded edge. Adjust the first ruler so it is flush with the second ruler. The goal here is to ensure that the first cut is at right angles to the fold, eliminating V-shaped strips.

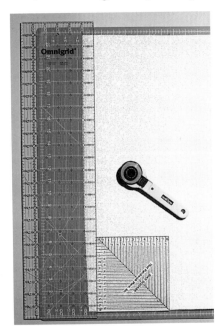

3. Hold the ruler securely in place and move the second ruler aside. Cut from below the fold to beyond the selvages in one clean, firm stroke.

You can now cut accurate strips from the clean-cut edge. Place the ruler on the fabric, with the desired strip-width marking on the cut edge of the fabric. Place a horizontal line on the fold again to ensure a right-angle cut. Cut the strip from bottom to top, away from yourself, rolling the rotary cutter along the edge of the ruler.

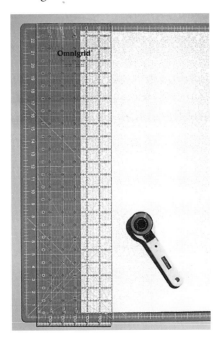

Now you are ready to crosscut squares and rectangles from strips of fabric. Squares can be further cut into half-square and quarter-square triangles as shown in the photo. Cut a square once diagonally to produce two half-square triangles with the bias grain on their long edges. Cut a square twice diagonally to make four quarter-square triangles with the straight grain on their long edges. The type of triangle you cut depends on the grain-line requirements of your project.

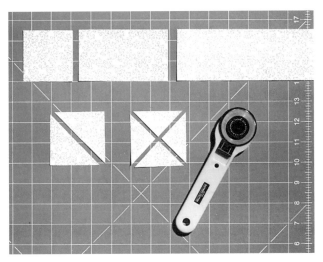

To cut diamonds from strips of fabric, make a template of the diamond shape. Tape it to the rotary ruler with the edge of the diamond on the cutting edge of the ruler. Cut strips as usual, using the width of the diamond as the cutting measurement.

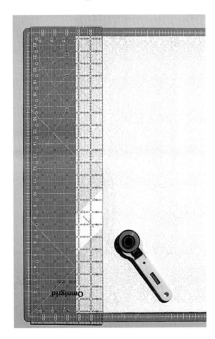

Once the strips are cut, use the template to slice diamonds from the fabric strips.

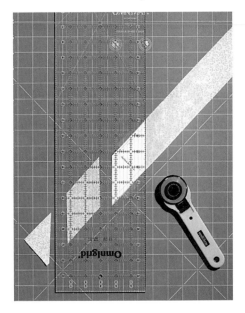

Strip Piecing

There are two types of strip piecing you will encounter frequently: straight-grain strip piecing and bias strip piecing. Both involve sewing strips together and cutting them into presewn shapes or units. They are different in that they use strips cut on different grain lines to accomplish their goals. You can gain a good deal of speed and accuracy by using strip-piecing techniques.

STRAIGHT-GRAIN STRIP PIECING

This technique eliminates the need to cut and sew individual squares and rectangles. Cut straight-grain strips from selvage to selvage, sew them together into strip units, and press them. Since the strips are cut from the cross grain, they can curve if not handled gently. For this reason, some people find it easier to work with half-length strips (21") instead of the full selvage-to-selvage length.

To cut segments from the strip unit, you must first trim one end of the strip unit so that it is even. Cut segments by measuring from the even edge; align a horizontal line of the ruler on one of the seams to make sure each cut is at right angles to the seams. The simple Nine Patch block is a good example.

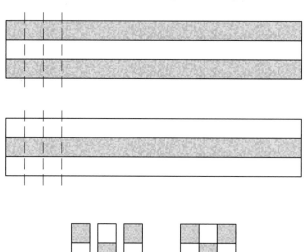

BIAS STRIP PIECING

Bias strip piecing is similar to straight-grain strip piecing except that the strips are cut on the bias. The simplest application of bias strip piecing is to make bias squares. These are squares composed of two right triangles sewn together along their long bias edges. Bias squares cut from strip units with bias edges will have the straight grain on their outside edges.

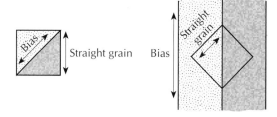

It is easiest to cut bias strips from rectangular pieces of fabric, but first, you must create a bias edge from which to cut the strips. Reverse the following directions and work from right to left if you are left-handed.

To make the bias cut:
1. Measure the height of the fabric from the lower left corner to the top edge of the fabric. Measure the same distance along the lower edge from the lower left corner and make a mark as shown. Make a diagonal cut from the mark to the upper left corner. Cut all fabrics for the same strip unit with the right side facing in the same direction, either all face up or all face down.

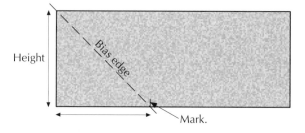

2. Working from left to right, cut bias strips from the bias edge. Do not cut into the corner triangle on the right side at this time. The strips you have cut are called *full bias strips* because they run from the top of the fabric to the bottom. The first and last cuts create large corner triangles. Sometimes, on wider pieces of fabric, corner triangles can be cut into corner bias strips and sewn into the strip unit too.

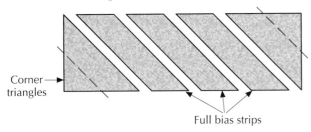

Corner → triangles

Full bias strips

To sew the bias strips into a strip unit:

1. Arrange the strips as indicated in the pattern.

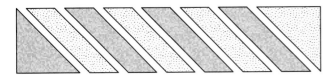

2. Offset the bias strips so the ¼" seam starts at the V. The top edge of the strip unit will be even.

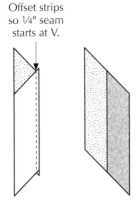

Offset strips so ¼" seam starts at V.

3. Sew the strips together in the same direction, from top to bottom, so the offset points are at the top of the strip unit. The bottom edge will be uneven.

4. To avoid stretching, don't hold or tug on the strips when sewing. See "Blue Ribbon Stitching Techniques" on pages 22–25 for lots of careful stitching ideas.

5. Sew slowly. Speed makes it harder to keep bias edges aligned.

6. Press each pair of strips before joining them into larger groups; they will be impossible to press en masse later without severe stretching. Refer to "Pressing" on page 17 for guidelines on pressing bias edges.

To cut bias squares from the bias-strip unit:

1. Arrange the strip unit on the cutting mat, right side up, with the top, even edge toward you. Place the diagonal line of the Bias Square ruler on the first seam, on the right-hand side of the strip unit, with the required bias-square dimensions inside the bottom raw edge. If your strip unit slants to the right, you will work from the left side of the strip unit.

2. Cut the top and side of the first bias square as shown, removing it from the strip unit. Turn the bias square around and cut the two remaining raw edges, trimming it to size.

3. Continue cutting bias squares in rows across the strip unit.

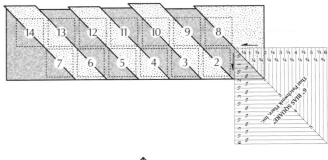

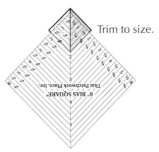

Trim to size.

Pressing

FOLLOWING A PRESSING PLAN

There are two primary reasons for pressing in a particular direction: 1) so your completed block or quilt will lie flat and smooth; and 2) so the seams will lie in opposite directions (butt) at intersections, making it easier to match them for stitching. The least important consideration is pressing toward the darker fabric as we have been taught in the past. This is a luxury choice you can make if the first two considerations have been met.

Just as with a car trip, it is nice to have the route mapped out in advance to avoid mistakes and wrong turns along the way. To avoid guesswork, it is a good idea to make a pressing plan before starting. Be aware, though, that sometimes there is just no such thing as a perfect pressing plan where everything works out exactly. In such cases, the only solution is a best effort.

Begin by making a scale drawing of your block(s) or quilt design. Include any pieced blocks, sashing strips, or borders that will butt against other pieced areas. Let's use the Nine Patch block as an example. To successfully butt seams and evenly distribute the seam allowances, you must press the squares in one of two ways. The first way is to press all the seams in rows 1 and 3 in one direction and the seams in row 2 in the opposite direction. The other way is to press all the seams toward the dark squares since they alternate. The seams that join the rows of blocks can be pressed in either direction.

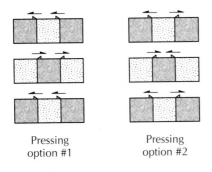

Pressing option #1   Pressing option #2

If the Nine Patch block will be positioned next to another pieced block, then the direction to press the seams where the two blocks meet is an important consideration when making a pressing plan and may necessitate changes. Depending on the pressing needs of the adjoining block, you may end up favoring one way of pressing the Nine Patch over another.

The process is the same for any block. Figure the most logical plan for the block. If it sits alone, you're done, but if it sits next to other pieced units, the pressing must be adjusted to fit the adjoining seams. Don't forget that there are four sides to the block. Unless the seams on each of the four sides are pressed exactly alike, then all four sides must be worked out individually.

Pressing directions have been determined for the quilt plans in this book. They are indicated by arrows or "ears" in each diagram where pressing is required. Occasionally, arrows would be awkward or unclear, and the directions are given in the written instructions. Look for and follow the pressing directions for ease of assembly and accuracy while stitching.

PRESSING SEAMS

A properly pressed seam is cleanly and crisply pressed to one side, without any pleats, distortions, or puckering on the right side. Here are a few tips that will help you.

- Press, don't iron. Ironing is an aggressive back-and-forth motion that we use on clothing to remove wrinkles. This action can easily pull and distort the bias edges or seams in your piecing. Perfectly marked and sewn quilt pieces are commonly distorted by an overly aggressive iron. Pressing is the gentle lowering, pressing, and lifting of the iron along the length of a seam. Let the heat do the work.
- Use a dry iron on the cotton setting. Steam distorts.

- Always press the seam line flat after sewing. This relaxes the thread, eases out any puckers from the stitching, and smooths out any fullness you may have eased in as you stitched. Try this and you'll be surprised at how nicely the seam will turn when you press it to one side.

- Arrange the fabric toward which you are pressing on top, with the open edges of the fabric pieces toward you and the stitched seam away from you. Use the tip of the iron to carefully open the unit, exposing the right side, then gently press the top fabric over the seam allowance. If a particular seam does not lie flat and crisp after pressing, use a spray bottle to mist it, then gently press it dry to provide a nice crease.

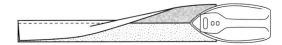

- To correct mistakes in pressing, return the unit to its original unpressed position and press the seam flat to remove the crease. A particularly crisp seam may need a spritz of water to relax the crease. Once you have removed the original crease, the seam can be pressed in the new direction with relative ease.

Press seam flat.

- When pressing bias seams, do not move the iron along the bias grain, but rather at a 45° angle to the seam along the straight grain. Many a seam is distorted and stretched by pressing along the bias.

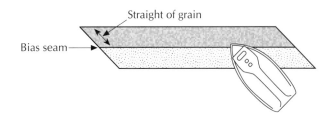

Straight of grain

Bias seam

Basic Stitching

STITCHING AN ACCURATE SEAM ALLOWANCE

The standard seam allowance for quiltmaking is ¼" wide. Seam allowances are added to template and rotary-cut pieces in different ways.

When working with finished-size templates, you draw lines around the template onto the fabric. These are the actual sewing lines. Add seam allowances when you cut the pieces by either drawing a precise cutting line ¼" from the sewing lines or roughly cutting ¼" from the sewing lines. Either way is fine, since the sewing lines must be aligned and pinned before sewing the pieces together. The cutting lines and size of the seam allowance are superfluous, but the sewing lines must be accurate for the pieces to fit together.

When working with rotary-cut pieces or cut-size templates, you include the seam allowances in the dimensions of the cut pieces. In this case, you align the raw edges of the pieces and sew a seam ¼" from the cut edges. Due to the absence of marked sewing lines, the cut sizes must be accurate, and an accurate ¼"-wide seam is necessary for the pieces to fit together. If the seam is too wide, the finished sizes of the pieces will be too small. Conversely, if the seam is too narrow, the finished sizes of the pieces will be too large. Both instances will result in inaccuracy and frustration as pieces refuse to fit together easily.

Many people assume that the edge of the presser foot is an accurate ¼"-wide seam guide. This is not always the case, so it is best to check your presser foot or the ¼" guide on your machine before you begin stitching. Use the following simple strip test to determine the accuracy of your guide. Do not assume that your machine is accurate unless you have done a strip test before. Adjusting the guide, if necessary, will save you a lot of frustration.

1. Cut 3 strips of fabric, each 1½" x 3".
2. Sew the strips together, using the edge of the presser foot or the ¼"-wide seam guide on the throat plate of your machine. Press seams away from the center strip.

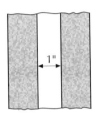

Center strip should measure a perfect 1" from seam to seam.

After sewing and pressing, the center strip should measure exactly 1" wide. If not, you must adjust the guide on your machine. Often, the center strip is narrower than 1", which means the seam allowance is wider than ¼". To create a new guide, try using a different presser foot or shifting the needle position to the right. Many machines now have a special ¼"-wide presser foot for quilters. Check with your local dealer or quilt shop for availability.

Zigzag machines with numerous needle positions can usually be adjusted to sew an accurate seam, with the edge of the presser foot as a guide. Shift your needle position to the right until you find the location that results in an accurate strip test.

If these options are unavailable to you, make a new guide with masking tape. Lift the presser foot and raise the unthreaded needle to its highest position. Cut out a 2" x 6" piece of ¼" graph paper. Be sure to cut accurately on the grid lines. Put the piece of graph paper under the presser foot and lower the needle into the graph paper just to the right of the first ¼" grid line from the right edge of the paper. Adjust the paper so it runs in a straight line from the needle and is not slanted to the left or right. Lower the presser foot to hold the paper in place. Use a piece of tape to hold the left edge of the paper so it doesn't slip.

Place a piece of masking tape along the right edge of the graph paper as shown. Make sure it is in front of and out of the way of the feed dogs.

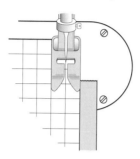

Test this new guide with the strip test described on page 18. If the guide is not accurate, readjust it until you can sew an accurate strip test several times in a row. Once it is accurate, build up the guide with several layers of tape to create a ridge you can use to guide the edge of the fabric. A piece of adhesive-backed mole-skin or foam also makes a good fabric guide.

ALIGNING THE PIECES

Machine piecing is the process of joining two pieces of fabric together with a straight running stitch. Pieces must be properly aligned before stitching. There are differences between sewing pieces with marked seam lines and with unmarked seam lines.

With *marked sewing lines*, place the fabric pieces to be matched right sides together. Use a pin to pierce the corner markings exactly at each end of the seam line of the top fabric, then run the pin exactly through the corner markings on the bottom piece. Secure the corners by running the pins through the fabric vertically.

Pin corners exactly.

Every inch or so, align the stitching line in the same fashion, using vertically placed pins. Check to make sure each pin pierces both lines exactly, front and back. Vertical pins keep the fabric from shifting horizontally. I run every other pin horizontally on the stitching line so I am sure the stitching lines are aligned along the length of the seam rather than only at specific pin points. This keeps the fabric from shifting vertically.

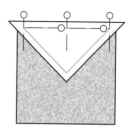

Place pins on the sewing line to secure.

With *unmarked sewing lines*, you do not need to pin. If you have included ¼"-wide seam allowances when you cut out your pieces, carefully align the cut edges before you stitch. Pins are rarely used to secure the edges before stitching except in special circumstances.

Trimming the points of triangles, diamonds, and other odd shapes that extend past the seam allowances makes it easier to align edges precisely. This is commonly called *nubbing*.

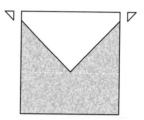

Nubbing before sewing
ensures better matching.

It's easy to nub half- and quarter-square triangles with the Bias Square ruler. For *half-square triangles*, add ½" to the finished size of the short side. Starting from the square corner, measure this distance and trim off the excess at each point as shown.

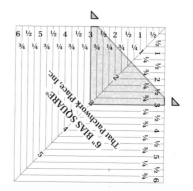

For *quarter-square triangles*, add ¼" to *half* of the finished size of the long edge. Press the triangle in half and measure this distance to the points opposite the fold. Trim the excess. Do not trim the folded edge.

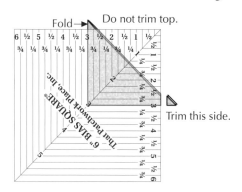

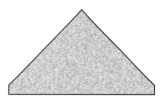

For odd-size pieces, use paper templates to make a nubbing guide. Draft the finished-size pieces on graph paper. Add ¼"-wide seam allowances on all sides. Cut out the paper pieces and align them on the sewing lines as if you were going to sew them together. Trim the excess paper extending past the points, then use the nubbed paper guides to nub the fabric pieces accordingly.

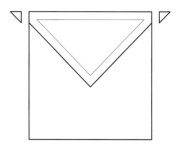

Align paper cutting guides
and trim points.

STITCHING

Machine-stitched seams are usually sewn from raw edge to raw edge. Backstitching is normally unnecessary because each seam will be crossed by another, locking the stitches in the process. However, there are a few special seams where it is important to leave the seam allowances free, and you must backstitch these seams. See "Backstitching" below.

When stitching on a marked sewing line, make sure the needle is in the center position and will pierce the stitching line. Sew from raw edge to raw edge without backstitching, removing the pins as you stitch.

When stitching without a sewing line, stitch from raw edge to raw edge, carefully guiding the aligned, cut edges of the pieces along the ¼" seam guide. Do not backstitch.

No matter which method you use, sew slowly and carefully; it's not a race. Fast stitching is usually sloppy stitching, resulting in inaccuracies and frustration. Take the time and care to do it right.

Be careful not to tug or pull on the fabric as it feeds through the machine; guide it but don't exert any pressure on it, or you may distort the pieces. Next to forceful pressing, "force feeding" your machine is probably the most common cause of misshapen triangles and squares.

BACKSTITCHING

It is necessary to backstitch when stitching from point to point. To backstitch normally, you would begin sewing exactly at the point, stitch forward for a few stitches, backstitch, and then proceed forward along the seam. Unfortunately, when you use this method, you must guess at just how far to stitch backward before you hit the corner, since the point is covered by the back of the presser foot.

To solve the problem, place the pieces you are sewing so the seam allowance is to the left of the needle and begin stitching on the sewing line, about ¼" from the corner. (If you do not have a sewing line, draw cross hairs at the intersection. See "Set-In Seams" on page 27.) Sew to the corner; stop precisely at the corner with the needle in the down position. Lift the presser foot and rotate the fabric back to its normal position, with the seam allowance to the right of the needle. Stitch along the remainder of the seam to the opposite point, where you can backstitch normally since you have full view of the point at all times.

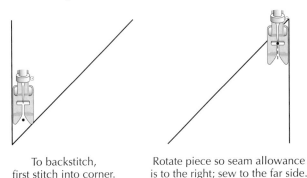

To backstitch, first stitch into corner.

Rotate piece so seam allowance is to the right; sew to the far side.

MATCHING INTERSECTIONS

The best way to tightly match the intersection of two seams is to press the seam allowances in opposite directions. This way, each of the seam allowances forms a ridge, and they can be pushed tightly against each other and sewn. This is called butting the seams.

Pieces with marked sewing lines are butted, but must also be matched along the sewing lines with pins as described earlier. Pin the corners first, then butt the matching seams and pin them securely on either side of the intersection. Stitch the seam as you normally would, sewing slowly and carefully.

To sew pieces with unmarked sewing lines and seam allowances included, first butt the seams at the intersections and then align the cut edges on the remainder of the seam. Except where noted in special circumstances, pins are generally not used to secure the intersection; the tightly aligned ridge of the seams does the job quite well. Sew slowly and carefully.

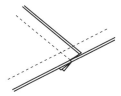

Butt straight seams.

When working with diagonal seams that must meet at a corner, be sure to press the seams in opposite directions so they butt tightly where they meet.

TIP

When stitching any corner where seams intersect, always start the stitching at the corner. This way, you can lock in the accuracy of the corner right from the start; the corner can easily be shifted out of alignment if it's the last area sewn. See "Blue Ribbon Stitching Techniques" on pages 22–25 for lots of tricks to help make the job easier and more accurate.

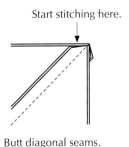

Start stitching here.

Butt diagonal seams.

CHECKING, TRIMMING, AND PRESSING

Check every seam after it is sewn to make sure you have sewn it correctly. It is much easier to make corrections now. Take out and restitch any seams or intersections that don't meet, and check the measurements of the units you've sewn. Interior pieces should be the finished size, while outer pieces should have one ¼"-wide seam allowance along the outer edge. If pieces are too small or too large, find out why and fix the problem now before it snowballs.

Trim every seam and press it immediately after sewing. Trimming is especially important for pieces that have not been cut with exact ¼"-wide seam allowances. Trim the seam to ¼" before you sew across it in the next step; also trim off any points extending beyond the seam allowance. Pieces with seam allowances included generally don't need trimming, except for a few points now and then.

Press all seams after sewing according to the pressing plan. See "Pressing Seams" on pages 16–17 for detailed information on how to press.

Blue Ribbon Stitching Techniques

Accuracy and attention to detail results in a beautifully made quilt. There is no single magic trick that will ensure perfection, but taking the time to be careful and finishing each step before proceeding to the next helps to increase the accuracy of your piecing. It also eliminates the frustration of trying to sew pieces together that don't quite match up. Here are a few little tips and tricks to add to your sewing repertoire. They will make a difference in how quickly and accurately your quilts go together.

STITCHING WITH SCRAP LEADS

This is a nifty little trick I learned in a class with Jeannette Muir. Rather than starting your stitching at the edge of the pieces, begin by sewing across a folded 1"- to 2"-wide strip of fabric that is the same weight as the fabric you are sewing (quilt-weight cotton for quilts). Leave the needle down in the forward edge of the strip and do not lift the presser foot. Clip the thread tails at the back of the strip, then position the seam you want to sew under the presser foot, about ⅛" in front of the scrap lead. You are now ready to sew the seam.

Scrap lead

When you have finished sewing the seam or a continuous chain of seams (see "Chain Sewing" on page 23), don't remove your fabric right away. Leave the needle down in the end of the last seam and sew across a second folded scrap. Stop with the needle down in the front of this scrap and clip the last units you sewed from the thread twist at the back. With the needle down in the second scrap, you are now ready for the next batch of sewing. Reuse the scrap leads over and over until they are covered with stitching. I save leftover lengths of fabric strips and keep them in a little basket by my sewing machine for just this purpose.

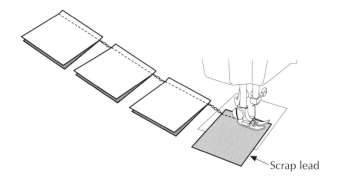
Scrap lead

There are several advantages to this trick. The most obvious is that you will no longer have thousands of little thread tails all over your work area. The scrap lead can also help alleviate the problem of the machine "eating" the fabric as you start a seam. With the scrap lead between the feed dogs and presser foot, the machine seems to feed the fabric through more smoothly. For those machines that tend to produce a few rough stitches as the stitching begins, the scrap lead absorbs these stitches so you have better stitch quality in the seam, where it counts.

One final advantage is the protection the scrap lead can provide for pointed pieces. When preparing to sew triangles, bias strips, or other pointed shapes, place the aligned points just on top of the scrap lead so they are protected by the scraps and are not sucked into the bobbin. If you are careful, you can lay the points on the scrap and still leave a gap between the scrap and the seam so they are not sewn together. When chain sewing a number of pointy pieces, place the points of the next set over the tail end of the previous set to protect all the points.

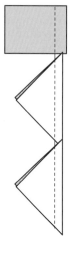

Chain Sewing

Chain sewing is an assembly-line approach to stitching. The idea is to save time by sewing as many seams as possible, one right after the other, rather than stopping and starting after each unit.

Begin a stretch of chain sewing with the scrap lead, followed by the first unit. Stop at the edge of the finished seam, but do not raise the needle, lift the presser foot, or remove the unit from the machine. Prepare the next unit for sewing, lift the presser foot slightly, and slip the unit underneath, leaving a small space between the sewn unit and the new one. Lower the presser foot and stitch.

Continue sewing in this same fashion with all the units, ending with a scrap lead. Clip the chain of units from behind the scrap lead, leaving the lead in the machine for your next stretch of sewing. You should now have a long "kite-tail" of stitched units connected by small twists of thread. Cut the units apart and continue with the next construction step.

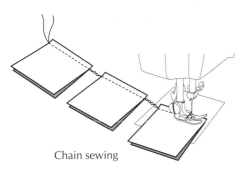

Chain sewing

Using the "Better Finger"

Sometimes our fingers are too big and clumsy for the close work we do with machine piecing. Try using a seam ripper or other slender, pointed instrument as a "better finger" to gently and accurately guide the fabric right up to the needle. Use it to hold intersections with pinpoint accuracy and make minute adjustments more easily than is possible with fingers.

It's also the ideal way to maintain a hands-off approach when sewing strips into strip units—especially bias strips, where stretching is a big problem.

When we use our hands to hold the strips, we unconsciously exert backward pressure on the strips. With the seam ripper, we guide the strips without the extra handling that can stretch them.

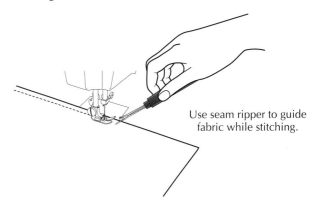

Use seam ripper to guide fabric while stitching.

Point-to-Point Sewing

Many seams involve matching and butting several intersections across the length of the seam. Check to make sure all seams will butt properly before starting to stitch. But instead of trying to keep all the seams matched at once, butt and sew just to and across the first intersection, then stop with the needle down in the seam. Before proceeding, butt the seams of the next intersection and use your seam ripper to hold them securely in place as they move up to the needle. Use this point-to-point system for sewing all the intersections along the entire length of the seam.

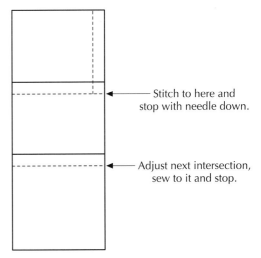

Stitch to here and stop with needle down.

Adjust next intersection, sew to it and stop.

Whether butting simple or intricate seams, stitching to match at seam intersections is easier if the open side of the seam allowance on the top layer faces the needle. The tendency for the top layer of fabric to be pushed forward will ensure a tight intersection, since the top seam ridge will be stopped by and forced more tightly into the ridge of the bottom seam allowance.

When the top seam allowance faces away from the needle, it can be pushed away from the intersection, causing a gap. When you have a choice, face the top seam toward the needle. Otherwise, use your seam ripper to keep the ridges tightly together.

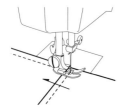

Face top seam allowance
toward needle.

SEWING FROM THE SQUARE

Whenever you are sewing a triangle to a square, it is always best to turn the seam so you begin stitching from the right-angle corner instead of the pointed triangle side. The feed dogs can handle the point better when it follows a seam than when it starts a seam. Use this same technique in similar situations.

Start stitching
from square corner.

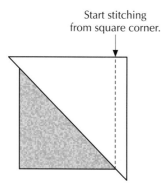

USING THE X

Unless you sew only squares and rectangles, you will eventually encounter a seam with a triangle or other intersection that you must sew across precisely. If you sew too far in from the cut edge, you will decapitate the point, and if you sew too close to the cut edge, the point will float. If you have been careful up to now, the point where the seams intersect in an X configuration should measure ¼" from the cut edge. If it does not, find out what went wrong and fix it. The ¼" seam you sew should intersect the X precisely to create an accurate point on the right side. Use the X as your guide whenever crossing a seam that should form a precise point at the ¼" seam mark.

The X intersection

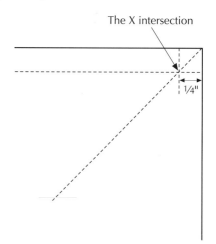

¼"

USING POSITIONING PINS

There are instances where you must match two or more intersections at one point on a seam. At times like this, using the X is not enough.

Use a pin to precisely spear the points on each of the two seams being matched. Leave this positioning pin upright in the fabric; do not secure it in the layers as you would normally. Instead, place a pin on either side of the upright pin to secure the seam so it does not shift. Sew the seam toward the positioning pin, removing other pins as you reach them. Sew slowly and carefully up to the positioning pin and remove it just before stitching across the intersection.

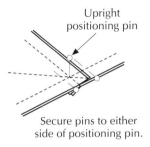

Upright
positioning pin

Secure pins to either
side of positioning pin.

PARTIAL BASTING

Partial basting is a handy technique for situations where butting seams is not possible. An example is matching a vertical seam and a diagonal seam. When the intersecting seams are placed right sides together for stitching, the different seams run in opposite directions, making alignment difficult.

Positioning pins can be used to match all the intersecting seams, but with a heavily or closely pieced unit, this can result in too many pins for comfortable sewing. Also, too many pins can cause seam distortions as they tend to shift the fabric slightly when they are twisted and secured in the fabric layers. To solve the problem, spear each intersection with a positioning pin and then quickly secure it with a hand-basting stitch. Remove the pins and machine stitch. Remove the hand basting after the seam is sewn.

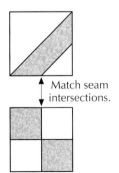

Match seam
intersections.

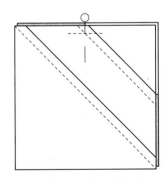

Spear intersection with pin.

EASING

Like it or not, there are times when it's necessary to ease in a little extra fullness in a seam. If there is a great deal of excess fabric on one seam, the source of the problem should be corrected. Use easing to correct small discrepancies, not large problems. Small bubbles are easy to ease in, but more then ¼" is not and must be corrected.

Easing is best done by stitching with the excess fullness on the bottom layer. In the case of a very tiny excess on a short seam with butted intersections, pinning is unnecessary as long as butting and the point of a seam ripper can hold all of the pieces in place while you stitch. If the seam is long, use pins to evenly distribute the excess along the length of the seam so there isn't any bunching at one particular point.

1. Begin by placing pins at the outer edges of the seam; then place a pin in the middle of the seam, arranging half the excess on each side of the pin.
2. Place a pin in the middle of each half, again dividing the excess between the two halves.
3. Keep pinning and dividing the excess until the fullness is evenly distributed and eased in with the pins. When the pinning is complete, you should barely be able to tell there's any fullness. If you can, you may want to reconsider correcting the source of the problem instead of easing it in. The result of easing in too much fullness is a heavily puckered seam, unsightly distortion, and continued problems with matching.

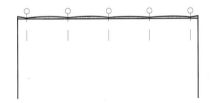

Ease fullness evenly along the seam, using pins.

4. Sew with the excess on the bottom so the feed dogs can "walk" in the excess. If the fuller seam is placed on top, the presser foot has a tendency to push the excess into pleats rather than ease it in.

Special Seams

DIAMONDS AND OTHER CENTRAL INTERSECTIONS

An eight-pointed star is one of the most intimidating piecing situations that a quilter faces. Stitching this block accurately takes a bit of care and a little practice, but in the end, it really is a "toothless dragon." I have tried several different methods for machine piecing stars and have found that the most successful one is based on the hand-piecing method I teach beginners. The key is to sew from point to point and to press the seams in a circular fashion so they not only butt when you are stitching, but also lie perfectly flat when completed. Add any squares, triangles, or other set-in shapes last. Let's use the traditional LeMoyne Star as an example for this technique.

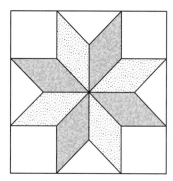

LeMoyne Star

1. If you are working without marked sewing lines, mark the ¼" cross hairs at all four corners of each diamond. Use the method described for "Set-in Seams" on page 27.

2. Arrange the diamonds as they will be assembled.

3. Pin the diamonds together in pairs along their adjoining seam. Pin points exactly, then sew from the center point to the outer point, backstitching at each end as described in "Backstitching" on pages 20–21.

Pin diamonds into pairs.
Sew from the center out.

4. Press seams consistently, either clockwise or counterclockwise.

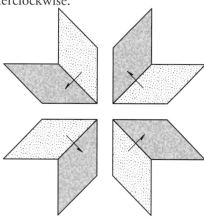

5. Join pairs of diamonds to form two star halves. Align the pairs by butting the seams. Sew from the center out, backstitching at the center intersection and pressing in a consistent circular fashion. Trim away the "ears" extending beyond the raw edge.

TIP

Check the center seam of each half before joining them. Make sure the points that meet in the center are ¼" from the raw edge. If it's more or less than ¼" from the edge to the point, figure out what you did wrong and correct it!

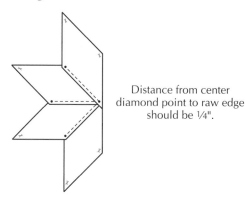

Distance from center diamond point to raw edge should be ¼".

6. Pin the two star halves together, using a positioning pin or partial basting to secure the center point. (See "Blue Ribbon Stitching Techniques" on pages 24–25.) The seams on each half should butt nicely. Pin the two outer points securely as well.

Secure center point with
upright positioning pin.

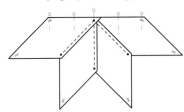

7. Sew the final seam to join the two halves, stitching from point to point. Despite the fact that this seam is sewn completely through the center point, you can still press in a circular fashion. When the pressing is complete, you should have a pin-wheel-type square formed by the seam allowances converging in the center.

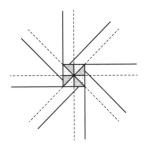

8. Set in any necessary pieces, following the directions for "Set-in Seams" below. Press the set-in seams in the same clockwise or counterclockwise direction as the diamond seams.

SET-IN SEAMS

Set-in seams are necessary when the only way to add a piece to a block is by stitching the piece into a corner in two stages. Diamond blocks frequently have set-in squares and triangles. Use the following guidelines when setting in squares, triangles, and all kinds of angled shapes.

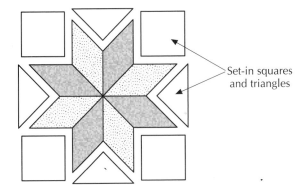

Set-in squares
and triangles

1. Mark the ¼" seam intersections at the outer corners and the inside corner of the pieces you are setting in. If you are working without a marked stitching line, use your ruler to measure and mark ¼" cross hairs at the seam intersections. Because you will be marking a sewing line on fabric that was cut without one, place the ¼" line of your ruler just *outside* the raw edge. If you measure with the ruler line *on* the fabric edge or just inside it, the pencil mark you make will actually be inside the finished area of your fabric piece, and the seam will be too wide.

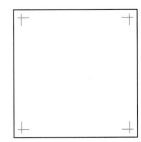

2. Begin by pinning only one side of the seam, being very careful to pin and match the corners exactly. Fold any pressed seams out of the way of the sewing area; pin, if necessary, to keep them out of the way.

3. Backstitch in the corner as described in "Backstitching" on pages 20–21, then stitch from the inside corner to the outer edge.

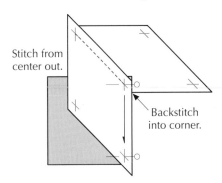

Stitch from center out.

Backstitch into corner.

If you are sewing all the way to the raw edge, backstitching is not necessary at the outer edge. If you are sewing from point to point on the outer edge, finish with a backstitch in the outer point.

4. Pin the other side of the seam and sew from the inside corner to the outer edge. Be very careful not to catch any part of the other seam or seam allowance when stitching the second side.

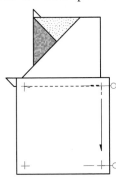

Twist second half of
seam into position;
pin at corners and
stitch from center out.

PARTIAL SEAMS

One way to avoid set-in seams in some cases is to use partial seams. Partial seams are used in situations where there is no clear-cut, patch-type assembly process. Usually this situation occurs where seams are built on each other in a circular fashion, returning at the end to the first seam. Look at the Hex Star block at right.

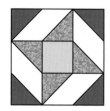

To avoid complicated piecing, sew just the first part of the first seam so the second one can be sewn in place normally. Each subsequent seam can then be sewn onto the previous seam. Looking at the block, you can see that if the first seam had been sewn completely, the last seam would have had to be set in. By sewing a partial seam first, there are no seams to set in. The last step is to go back and complete the remainder of the first seam. Backstitching is unnecessary as long as you stitch over the first stitching.

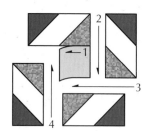
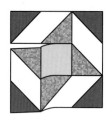

Sew second half of
first seam to finish block.

CURVED SEAMS

Curved seams are another type of seam that many quiltmakers tend to avoid. Happily, with a little bit of care, they are not that difficult. Every curved seam has two types of curves: convex and concave. My geometry teacher taught us how to remember which was which by describing the concave curve as the one you could walk into like a cave. Maybe that will help you remember, too.

When matching these two curves, you will notice that they are mirror images of each other and that the concave seam must be "stretched" to fit around the convex seam. This is done by clipping periodically into the concave seam allowance. There is no need to clip the convex seam. Clips

should not be any more than ⅛" deep into the seam allowance. It is better to put only a few clips into the seam at first and add more later, if needed, to create a smooth seam.

Make ⅛"-deep clips
along concave curves.

If your templates do not have center guidelines, make them yourself. Make a finished-size paper template and fold it in half to find the center of the seam. Use this guide to mark the center of the curved edge of each fabric piece.

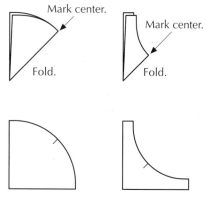

Use template to mark center of fabric piece.

Place a pin at the center of the seam, aligning the center guidelines. Place pins along the curved edges to keep them from slipping out of position.

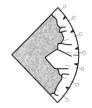

Pin concave piece
to convex piece with
center guidelines matching.

If you are working with pieces that have marked sewing lines, finish pinning the remainder of the seam as described on page 19.

When sewing lines are not marked, you may not need any more than three pins, one at each edge and one in the center, to sew a smooth and accurate seam. Sew slowly and carefully, aligning the raw edges as you go. Use more pins if you prefer. In general, you will probably need more pins for deep curves and fewer pins for gentle curves.

A curved seam will lie flatter, without pulls and puckers, if it is adequately clipped and pressed toward the concave piece. You may need to add a few extra clips here and there to help it lie flat.

continued on page 37

Gallery

MARBLED REFLECTIONS BY ROBIN CHAMBERS

1997, Media, Pennsylvania, 51½" x 51½". Even though this quilt looks like it is diagonally set, it is not. Robin used bright and beautiful marbleized prints to make each star, and a navy blue garden print for the triangles makes up the four corners of each block as well as the outer border. The result is a delightful quilt. Directions begin on page 54.

DOMINO BY DONNA LYNN THOMAS

1997, Peachtree City, Georgia, 64½" x 64½". Domino is a traditional block design that has many possibilities for both color and set. In this variation, bright blue and red crosses interlock across the quilt. The use of many prints makes the quilt exciting while keeping the assembly process quite simple. Machine quilted by Kari Lane. Directions begin on page 41.

PAINTERLY DOMINO BY ANN WOODWARD

1997, Collegeville, Pennsylvania, 64½" x 64½". A simple turn of the Domino block makes Ann's quilt look like a Trip Around the World. The beautiful purple and green batiks lend a soft, elegant look to her quilt.

TARTAN STARS BY DONNA LYNN THOMAS

1997, Peachtree City, Georgia, 38⅝" x 35⅝". Metallic plaid stars set on point with black side setting triangles and variegated metallic threads in the quilting make this quilt sparkle and dance—especially when caught by the light! Blocks made in pairs from different fabric combinations help keep it lively and also make it easy to increase the size of your quilt without a lot of fuss. Machine quilted by Kari Lane. Directions begin on page 46.

PACIFICA STARS BY DEE GLENN

1997, Lansing, Kansas, 47⅝" x 47⅝". Dee's stunning quilt is based on the multicolored batik print she used for the background in her blocks, the side setting triangles, and the outer border. She chose darker batik prints to make each pair of blocks and quilted all over with a meandering design for a beautiful finish.

Not to be forgotten, the back of Dee's quilt is just as dynamic as the front.

PRIMARY SQUARES BY KARI LANE

1997, Lawson, Missouri, 52½" x 52½". This beautiful quilt is a delight to the eyes and, oh, so simple to assemble. Choose a bright print and a dark print and make a pair of blocks; keep making pairs of blocks until you have as many blocks as you need. This pattern would be equally at home with traditional prints as with Kari's choices of batiks and hand-dyed fabrics. Directions begin on page 44.

PRIMARILY AFRICA BY KARI LANE

1997, Lawson, Missouri, 52½" x 63". Wild, wonderful, and fun is the way Kari likes her quilts, and these African prints fill the bill! Kari chose to use light prints for the bands through the blocks instead of the dark ones in "Primary Squares," and pieced both her borders from an assortment of prints.

DOUBLE ASTER
BY DONNA LYNN THOMAS

1997, Peachtree City, Georgia, 47½" x 47½". The burgundy, lavender, and gold of an autumn garden are reflected in this lovely wall hanging. A pieced sashing helps to soften the regimented straight set of the quilt. The traditional floral design quilted over the blocks gives a traditional and comforting feel to this quilt. Hand quilted by Judy Keller. Directions begin on page 49.

KEY WEST BEAUTY BY DEB ROSE

1997, Fort Leavenworth, Kansas, 43½" x 54½". Clear watermelon pink and antique green make a pretty combination for this old-time block. The curved seams in the corner of each block give the illusion of circles. A gorgeous border print frames the quilt with neat mitered corners. Directions begin on page 52.

continued from page 28

MITERED SEAMS

Mitered seams are diagonal seams that are sewn from an inner corner to an outer edge. A square-corner miter is the most common, although strips can also be mitered around such shapes as hexagons, octagons, and diamonds. Border corners are frequently mitered, as are some parts of pieced blocks. Mitering can be done with template-marked pieces or with rotary-cut strips.

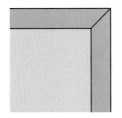 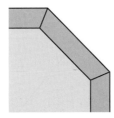

Strips sewn to quilt and mitered at the corner

Mitered corners around octagon

MITERING WITH TEMPLATES

If you are working with templates, the process of mitering is relatively simple. The angle of the mitered seam is determined by your drafted template. It is a matter of proper matching and sewing.

1. If you are working with templates that include seam allowances, use your ruler to mark the intersecting ¼" seam lines at the corners of both strips and the quilt top.

2. Pin the strips to the sides of the quilt, working carefully from point to point. Sew each seam exactly from corner to corner without stitching into the ¼" seam allowances. Do not press yet.

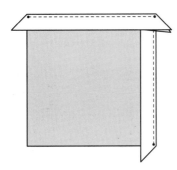

3. Fold the quilt top diagonally with wrong sides together. Align the unpressed seams and tails of the border strips, right sides together, as shown. Carefully pin the inside corner and the stitching line or raw edges of the mitered angle, depending on whether you have marked sewing lines or not. Backstitch, then sew exactly from the inside corner of the mitered seam to the outside corner on the stitching line; or sew a seam ¼" from the raw edge. Unfold the quilt top and mitered border to check the accuracy and flatness of the seam. Trim and press the seam carefully since it is a bias seam.

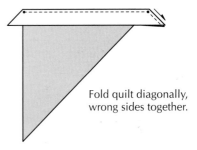

Fold quilt diagonally, wrong sides together.

MITERING WITH ROTARY-CUT STRIPS

Mitering with rotary-cut strips is essentially the same as mitering with templates, with a few small changes.

1. Cut the strips extra long to accommodate the miter. Calculate the length by adding the finished border length, plus twice the border width and two to three inches more for good measure. If several strips are to be mitered around a particular corner, seam them together first and miter them all at once. Remember that, in this case, the border width is the combined width of the seamed strips.

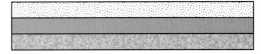

Sew strips together for a multiple border.

2. Make a mark ¼" from each corner of the quilt top. Center the border strip on the side of the quilt top, leaving enough excess strip width on either side to accommodate the strip width plus an inch or two more. Pin in place and sew exactly from marked corner to marked corner as in step 2 on page 37.

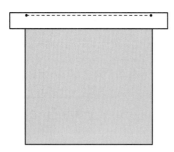

3. Fold the quilt top and arrange the strips on top of each other as in step 3 on page 37. Since the strips were rotary cut, there is no angled cut on the ends of the strips, making it necessary to mark them now. For right angles, you can also use the 45°-angle line on your rotary ruler to make the correct mark. See also "Making Your Own Mitering Guides" at right to make nonstandard angles.

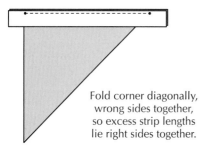

Fold corner diagonally, wrong sides together, so excess strip lengths lie right sides together.

4. Place the angled corner of the mitering guide (or ruler) at the point where the stitching stops at the corner. Draw a line along the edge of the guide from the stitching at the corner to the opposite raw edge of the fabric strip. Do this on both strips.

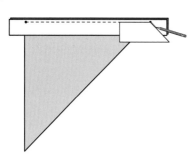

5. Pin the seam along the drawn lines, matching any seams or fabric designs that converge at the seam. Backstitch, then stitch exactly from the inside corner to the opposite raw edge.

6. Check the mitered seam for accuracy and flatness before trimming the excess, leaving a ¼"-wide seam allowance. Press the seam allowance to one side, being careful not to stretch the bias.

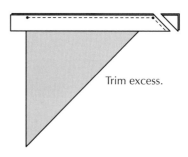

Trim excess.

MAKING YOUR OWN MITERING GUIDES

To miter around a corner with an odd angle, you need to make your own mitering guide. You will need graph paper, pencil, and a protractor. A protractor is a circle or half circle with cross hairs in the center and degree lines on the outer edge. It is used to measure angles from any given point.

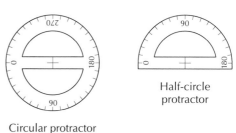

Circular protractor

Half-circle protractor

If you are working with fabric pieces that do not have a marked sewing line, draw 2" to 3"-long cross hairs ¼" from the corner to be measured.

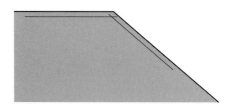

To measure the angle, place the cross hairs in the center of the protractor over the marked cross hairs or seam line on the corner of the fabric piece. Align the 0° mark along the seam line on one of the sides to be mitered. Now measure from 0° to the seam line on the other side to find the number of degrees in the angle.

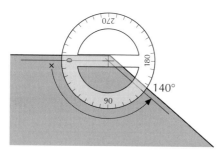

Measure from x
to opposite side of corner.

To determine the degree of the mitering angle:
1. Subtract the corner angle (determined above) from 360°.
2. Divide the result in half. This is the mitering angle.
   Example: The corner angle measures 140°. Subtract this from 360° and you get 220°. Divide 220° in half. The mitering angle is 110°.

To draw the mitering guide:
1. Draw a 6"-long horizontal line on a piece of graph paper. Mark the center of the line.

Center mark

2. Place the cross hairs of the protractor on the center point of the horizontal line, with 0° to the left and 180° to the right.
3. Measure from 0° to 110° (or whatever you've calculated for your mitering angle) in a counterclockwise direction. Mark the paper at this point. This is the mitering angle.

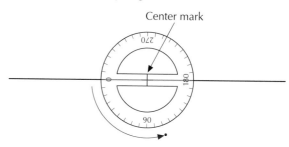

Measure from 0° counterclockwise
and mark the correct mitering angle.

4. Draw a line from the center point to the mark you just made. Make a template from the shaded area to the left of the line as shown. Use this guide to miter the corner.

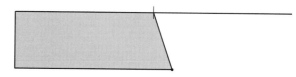

The Quilt Plans

There are six quilt plans included in this section. Five of them are written for both template-cut and rotary-cut techniques. The other, Key West Beauty, is written for template-cut quiltmaking only.

In all six plans, dimensions for all sashings, borders, and bindings include the ¼"-wide seam allowances. The fabric requirements for the dual-technique plans are sufficient for either method. Cutting instructions for both techniques are followed by general cutting instructions for items such as sashings and borders that are cut the same no matter which method you use.

Assembly instructions are written in a similar fashion, with special template-cut instructions first, followed by the rotary version. After the differences are dealt with, the assembly instructions apply to both techniques.

Pressing directions have been determined in advance and are indicated by arrows or "ears" in the diagrams or in the written instructions. Please be sure to look for and follow these instructions, since they will result in opposing seams at intersections.

Cutting instructions are based on fabric that measures no less than 40" wide from selvage to selvage after prewashing. If your fabric measures more than this, you may find you have some extra fabric or an occasional extra strip length. The reverse will be true if your fabric measures less than 40" wide after washing. Be aware of the fabric widths used by different manufacturers when you are selecting and purchasing fabric for a quilt. You can no longer assume 44"- to 45"-wide fabric is standard.

If you work through and make each of the six quilts in this section, you will have tried your hand at most of the techniques presented in *A Perfect Match*. Have fun!

DOMINO

Color Photo: page 30 ■ Finished Quilt Size: 64½" x 64½" ■ Finished Block Size: 9" x 9"

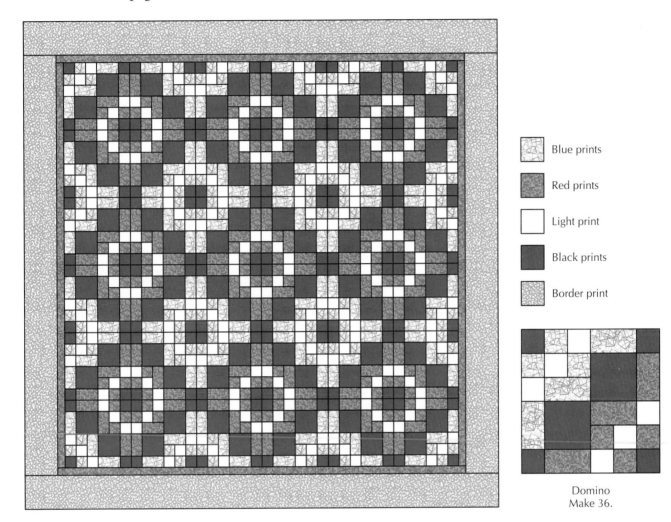

Blue prints

Red prints

Light print

Black prints

Border print

Domino
Make 36.

MATERIALS: 42"-WIDE FABRIC

1⅛ yds. (or 4 or more fat quarters) total assorted blue prints

1⅛ yds. (or 4 or more fat quarters) total assorted red prints

⅞ yd. light print

1⅜ yds. total assorted black prints

⅜ yd. red print for inner border

1 yd. multicolor print for outer border

4⅛ yds. for backing

71" x 71" piece of batting

½ yd. for binding

TEMPLATE CUTTING

Use Templates #2, #3, and #4 on page 62.
From the assorted red prints, cut:
   108 Template #2
   108 Template #3

From the assorted blue prints, cut:
   108 Template #2
   108 Template #3
From the light print, cut:
   216 Template #2
From the assorted black prints, cut:
   144 Template #2
   72 Template #4

ROTARY CUTTING

From the assorted blue prints, cut:
   12 strips, each 2" x 20"
   12 strips, each 3½" x 20"
From the assorted red prints, cut:
   27 strips, each 2" x 20"
   4 strips, each 3½" x 20"
From the light print, cut:
   24 strips, each 2" x 20"

From the assorted black prints, cut:
15 strips, each 3½" x 20"
16 strips, each 2" x 20"

CUTTING FOR BOTH METHODS

From the red print, cut:
6 strips, each 1½" x 40", for inner border
From the multicolor print, cut:
7 strips, each 4½" x 40", for outer border
From the binding fabric, cut:
7 strips, each 2" x 40"

BLOCK ASSEMBLY

Press all seams in direction of arrows unless otherwise instructed.

1. For *template construction*, assemble the assorted segments shown, using the red, blue, light, and black squares, and red and blue rectangles.

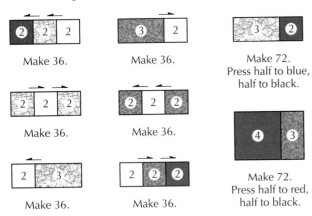

Make 36.

Make 36.

Make 72.
Press half to blue,
half to black.

Make 36.

Make 36.

Make 36.

Make 36.

Make 72.
Press half to red,
half to black.

For *rotary construction*, assemble strip units A–H as shown. Cut the number and sizes of segments indicated for each strip unit. After cutting segments from strip units G and H, readjust the pressing as necessary so that 36 segments are pressed in one direction and 36 in the other direction.

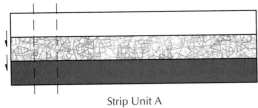

Strip Unit A
Make 4.
Cut 36 segments, each 2" wide.

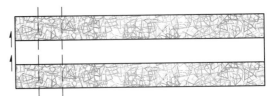

Strip Unit B
Make 4.
Cut 36 segments, each 2" wide.

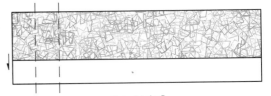

Strip Unit C
Make 4.
Cut 36 segments, each 2" wide.

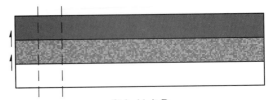

Strip Unit D
Make 4.
Cut 36 segments, each 2" wide.

Strip Unit E
Make 4.
Cut 36 segments, each 2" wide.

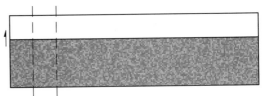

Strip Unit F
Make 4.
Cut 36 segments, each 2" wide.

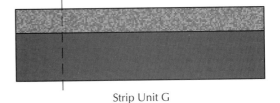

Strip Unit G
Make 15.
Press 7 strip units in one direction and 8 in the other.
Cut 72 segments, each 3½" wide.

Strip Unit H
Make 8.
Press 4 strip units in one direction and 4 in the other.
Cut 72 segments, each 2" wide.

2. Using the segments from step 1, assemble 36 of each of the 4 units shown.

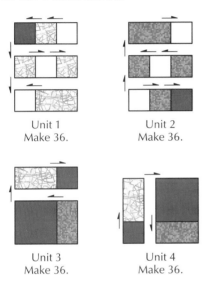

Unit 1
Make 36.

Unit 2
Make 36.

Unit 3
Make 36.

Unit 4
Make 36.

3. Arrange 1 of each unit as shown and sew them together to complete a Domino block. Make 36 blocks.

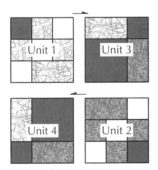

Unit 1 Unit 3

Unit 4 Unit 2

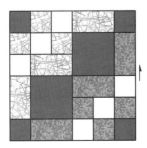

Domino
Make 36.

QUILT TOP ASSEMBLY AND FINISHING

1. Arrange the blocks in 6 rows of 6 blocks each. Experiment with different layouts to make different designs. Refer to the photos on pages 30 and 31 for two alternatives. Sew the blocks together in rows, pressing seams in opposite directions from row to row.

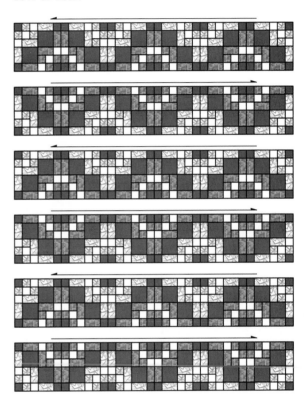

2. Join the rows, pressing seams in either direction.
3. Referring to "Plain Borders" on page 57 and the quilt plan on page 41, measure, cut, and add first the inner, then the outer borders.
4. Referring to "Finishing" on pages 57–61, layer the completed quilt top with batting and backing; baste.
5. Quilt as desired, then bind the edges. Label the quilt.

PRIMARY SQUARES

Color Photo: page 34 ■ Finished Quilt Size: 52½" x 52½" ■ Finished Block Size: 10½" x 10½"

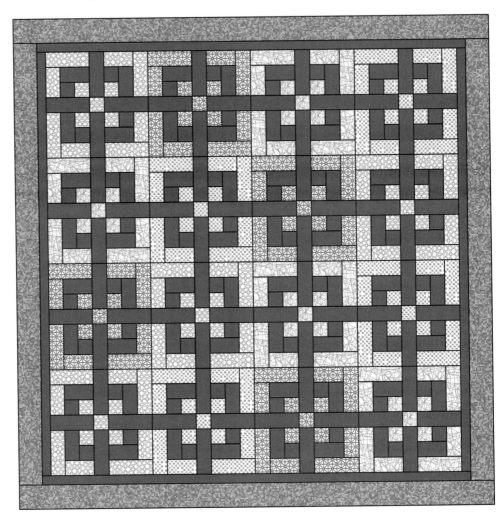

Navy blue prints

Bright prints

Border print

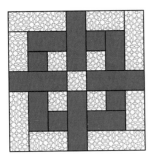

Primary Squares
Make 16.

MATERIALS: 42"-WIDE FABRIC

¼ yd. or 1 fat quarter *each* of 8 navy blue prints

¼ yd. or 1 fat quarter *each* of 8 bright prints

⅜ yd. dark print for inner border (or make a pieced border from leftover navy blue prints)

¾ yd. multicolor print for outer border

3½ yds. for backing

59" x 59" piece of batting

½ yd. for binding

TEMPLATE CUTTING

Use Templates #1, #2, and #3 on page 62.

From each of the 8 navy blue prints, cut:

8 Template #1

8 Template #2

8 Template #3

From each of the 8 bright prints, cut:

8 Template #1

10 Template #2

8 Template #3

ROTARY CUTTING

From each of the 8 navy blue prints, cut:
  8 pieces, each 2" x 5"
  8 pieces, each 2" x 3½"
  8 squares, each 2" x 2"
From each of the 8 bright prints, cut:
  8 pieces, each 2" x 5"
  8 pieces, each 2" x 3½"
  10 squares, each 2" x 2"

CUTTING FOR BOTH METHODS

From the dark print, cut:
  5 strips, each 2" x 40", for inner border

OPTIONAL: To make a pieced border, cut 20 strips, each 2" x 10", from the 8 leftover navy blue prints. Sew them together randomly to make one long strip and cut border strips from this.

From the multicolor print, cut:
  5 strips, each 4" x 40", for outer border
From the binding fabric, cut:
  5 strips, each 2" x 40"

BLOCK ASSEMBLY

The following instructions are for making 2 blocks from each navy blue/bright fabric combination. You will make a total of 16 blocks. *Press all seams in direction of arrows unless otherwise instructed.*

1. Sew a 2" bright square (Template #2) to a 2" navy blue square (Template #2). Make 8 pairs.

Make 8.

2. Arrange a pair of squares with the remaining bright and navy blue pieces as shown. Sew them together to complete a corner unit. Make 8 corner units.

Corner Unit
Make 8.

3. Join the corner units, 2" x 5" navy blue strips (Template #1), and 2" bright squares (Template #2) as shown. Make 2 blocks.

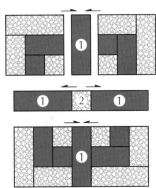

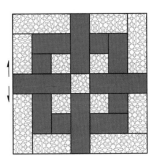

Primary Squares
Make 2.

4. Repeat steps 1–3 with the remaining navy blue/bright fabric combinations to make 16 blocks.

QUILT TOP ASSEMBLY AND FINISHING

1. Arrange the blocks in 4 rows of 4 blocks each, making sure the colors are balanced. Alternate the direction of the final two seams vertically and horizontally from block to block so seams will butt. Sew the blocks together into rows, pressing seams in opposite directions from row to row.

2. Join the rows, pressing seams in either direction.

3. Referring to "Plain Borders" on page 57 and the quilt plan on page 44, measure, cut, and add first the inner, then the outer borders.

4. Referring to "Finishing" on pages 57–61, layer the completed quilt top with batting and backing; baste.

5. Quilt as desired, then bind the edges. Label the quilt.

TARTAN STARS

Color Photo: page 32 ▪ Finished Quilt Size: 38⅝" x 38⅝" ▪ Finished Block Size: 9" x 9"

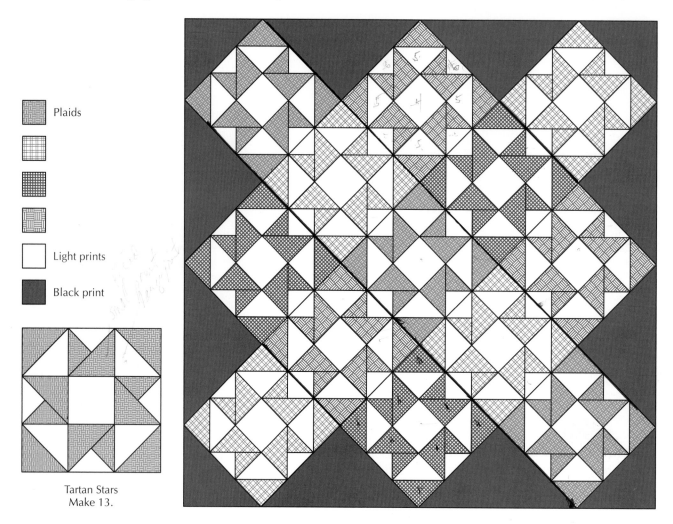

Plaids

Light prints

Black print

Tartan Stars
Make 13.

MATERIALS: 42"-WIDE FABRIC

1 fat quarter *each* of 7 plaids and 7 light prints
⅝ yd. black print
1⅜ yds. for backing
45" x 45" piece of batting
⅜ yd. for binding

TEMPLATE CUTTING

Use Templates #4, #5, and #6 on pages 62–64.
From each *of the plaids, cut:*
16 Template #5
8 Template #6
From each *of the light prints, cut:*
8 Template #5
8 Template #6
2 Template #4

ROTARY CUTTING

From each *of the plaids, cut:*
1 piece, 9" x 13½"; cut 1 full bias strip, 3⅛" wide,
from the piece. Reserve the 9" corner triangles.
2 squares, each 4¼" x 4¼"; cut each square twice
diagonally for 8 quarter-square triangles
4 squares, each 3⅞" x 3⅞"; cut each square once
diagonally for 8 half-square triangles
From each *of the light prints, cut:*
1 piece, 9" x 18"; cut 2 full bias strips, each 3⅛"
wide, from the piece
2 squares, each 3½" x 3½", for block centers
From the leftover 9" corner triangles, cut:
2 squares, each 4¼" x 4¼"; cut each square twice
diagonally for 8 quarter-square triangles

CUTTING FOR BOTH METHODS

From the black print, cut:
   2 squares, each 14½" x 14½"; cut each square twice diagonally for 8 side setting triangles
   2 squares, each 8" x 8"; cut each square once diagonally for 4 corner triangles
From the binding fabric, cut:
   4 strips, each 2" x 40"

BLOCK ASSEMBLY

The following instructions yield 2 blocks from each fabric combination. *Press all seams in direction of arrows unless otherwise instructed.*

1. For *template construction*, sew a light triangle (Template #5) to a plaid triangle (Template #5). Make 8. Press 4 toward the plaid triangle and 4 toward the light.

   Make 4.   Make 4.

For *rotary construction*, assemble a bias-strip unit as shown with the plaid and light full bias strips and the 2 reserved plaid 9" corner triangles. Referring to "Bias Strip Piecing" on pages 14–15, cut 8 bias squares, each 3½" x 3½", from the strip unit.

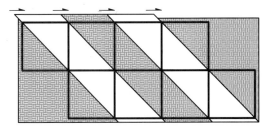

2. For both methods, sew the plaid and light quarter-square triangles (Template #6) into pairs. Press 4 toward the plaid triangle and 4 toward the light.

   Make 4.   Make 4.

3. Sew each triangle pair to a plaid half-square triangle (Template #5) to make 8 units. Press 4 toward the plaid triangle and 4 toward the triangle pair.

   Make 4.

   Make 4.

4. Assemble 2 Tartan Star blocks as shown, each pressed in opposite directions.

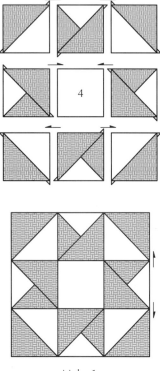

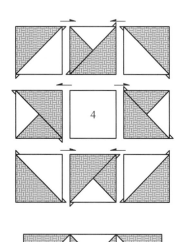

Make 1.

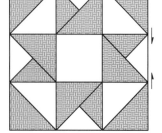

Make 1.

5. Repeat steps 1–4 to make 14 stars. You will have one extra star.

QUILT TOP ASSEMBLY AND FINISHING

1. Arrange 13 Tartan Star blocks with the side and corner setting triangles in a pleasing arrangement. Be sure to place blocks pressed in opposite directions next to each other so seams will butt. Sew the blocks and triangles into rows, pressing the seams in opposite directions from row to row.

2. Join the rows, pressing seams in either direction.
3. Referring to "Finishing" on pages 57–61, layer the completed quilt top with batting and backing; baste.
4. Quilt as desired, then bind the edges. Label the quilt.

DOUBLE ASTER

Color Photo: page 36 ■ Finished Quilt Size: 47½" x 47½" ■ Finished Block Size: 10" x 10"

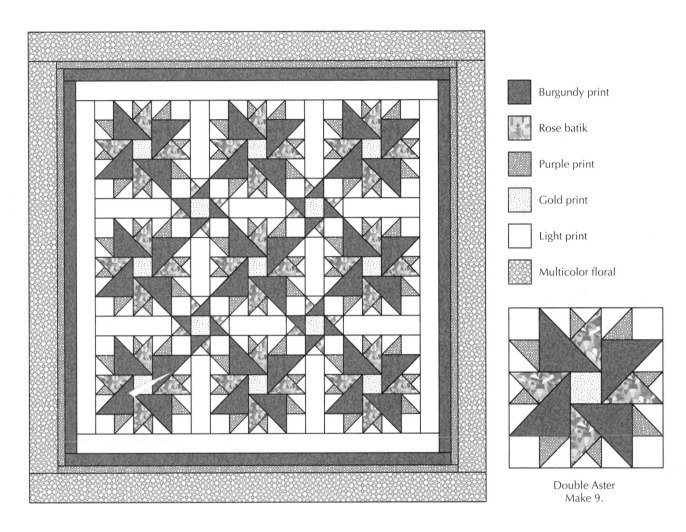

Burgundy print

Rose batik

Purple print

Gold print

Light print

Multicolor floral

Double Aster
Make 9.

MATERIALS: 42"-WIDE FABRIC

⅞ yd. burgundy print
½ yd. rose batik
¾ yd. purple print
⅛ yd. gold print
1⅜ yds. light print
⅝ yd. multicolor floral for outer border
3⅛ yds. for backing
54" x 54" piece of batting
⅜ yd. for binding

TEMPLATE CUTTING

Use Templates #7, #8, #9, #10, and #11 on pages 62–63.

From the burgundy print, cut:
  36 Template #8
  16 Template #11
From the rose batik cut:
  36 Template #9
  16 Template #10
From the purple print, cut:
  36 Template #11
  36 Template #10
From the gold print, cut:
  13 Template #7
From the light print, cut:
  36 Template #7
  52 Template #10
  72 Template #11

ROTARY CUTTING

From the burgundy print, cut:

18 squares, each 4⅞" x 4⅞"; cut each square once diagonally for 36 half-square triangles

8 squares, each 2⅞" x 2⅞"; cut each square once diagonally for 16 half-square triangles

From the rose batik, cut:

9 squares, each 5¼" x 5¼"; cut each square twice diagonally for 36 quarter-square triangles

4 squares, each 3¼" x 3¼"; cut each square twice diagonally for 16 quarter-square triangles

From the purple print, cut:

9 squares, each 3¼" x 3¼"; cut each square twice diagonally for 36 quarter-square triangles

1 piece, 9" x 30"; cut 6 full bias strips, each 2½" wide, from the piece. Reserve 1 corner triangle.

From the gold print, cut:

13 squares, each 2½" x 2½"

From the light print, cut:

1 piece, 9" x 30"; cut 6 full bias strips, each 2½" wide, from the piece. Reserve 1 corner triangle.

13 squares, each 3¼" x 3¼"; cut each square twice diagonally for 52 quarter-square triangles

18 squares, each 2⅞" x 2⅞"; cut each square once diagonally for 36 half-square triangles

36 squares, each 2½" x 2½"

CUTTING FOR BOTH METHODS

From the burgundy print, cut:

5 strips, each 1¾" x 40", for second border

From the purple print, cut:

5 strips, each 1¼" x 40", for third border

From the light print, cut:

8 strips, each 2½" x 8½", for sashings

4 strips, each 2½" x 6½", for sashings

4 strips each 2½" x 40", for inner border

From the multicolor floral, cut:

5 strips, each 3" x 40", for outer border

From the binding fabric, cut:

5 strips, each 2" x 40"

BLOCK ASSEMBLY

Press all seams in direction of arrows unless otherwise instructed.

1. For template construction, sew each purple half-square triangle (Template #11) to a light half-square triangle (Template #11) to make 36 bias squares.

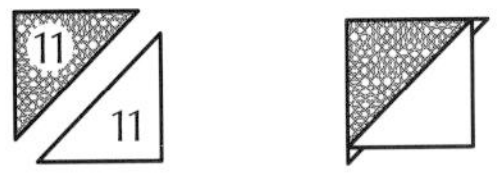

Make 36.

2. For rotary construction, cut the reserved purple and light 9" corner triangles into 2½"-wide corner bias strips. Using the full and corner bias strips, assemble a bias-strip unit as shown. Cut 36 bias squares, each 2½" x 2½".

2½"-wide corner bias strip

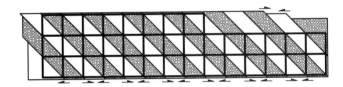

3. For both methods, arrange the light and purple quarter-square triangles (Template #10) and light half-square triangle (Template #11) as shown, then sew them together to complete a pieced triangle.

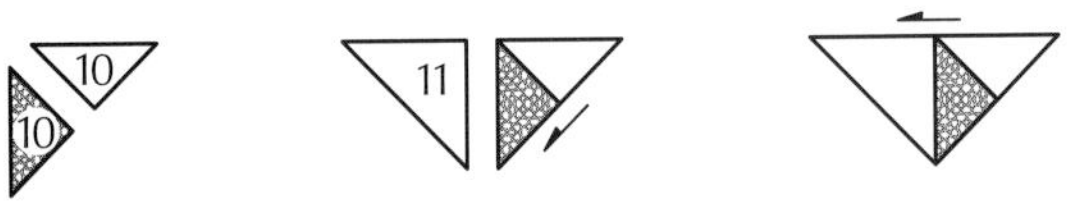

Pieced Triangle
Make 36.

4. Arrange the pieced triangles with the rose quarter-square triangles (Template #9) and burgundy half-square triangles (Template #8) as shown, then sew them together to complete a triangle unit.

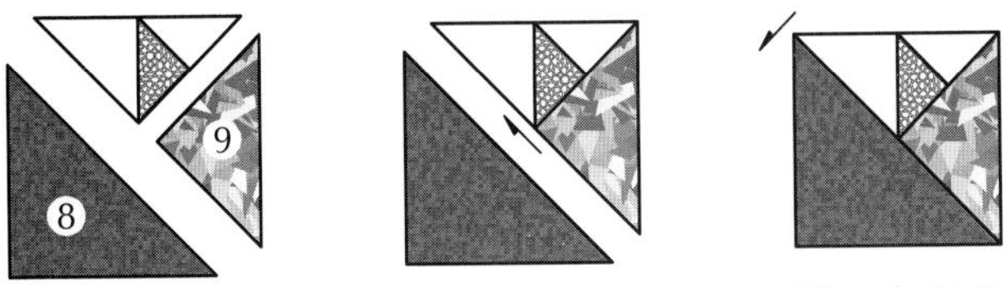

Triangle Unit
Make 36.

5. Sew each bias square created in step 1 or step 2 to a 2½" light square (Template #7). Stitch the completed unit to a triangle unit as shown to create a corner unit.

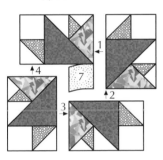

Corner Unit
Make 36.

6. Referring to "Partial Seams" on page 28, sew 4 corner units around a 2½" gold square (Template #7) to make a Double Aster block. Make 9 blocks.

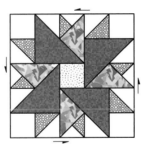

Double Aster
Make 9.

QUILT TOP ASSEMBLY AND FINISHING

1. Arrange the burgundy half-square triangles (Template #11) with the rose and light quarter-square triangles (Template #10) as shown, then sew them together to make the triangle units for the sashing.

Sashing Triangle Unit
Make 16.

2. Sew a triangle unit to one end of each 2½" x 8½" sashing strip. Sew a triangle unit to each end of each 2½" x 6½" sashing strip as shown.

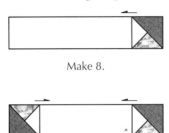

Make 8.

Make 4.

3. Arrange the blocks, sashing strips, and gold squares as shown, then sew them together in rows.

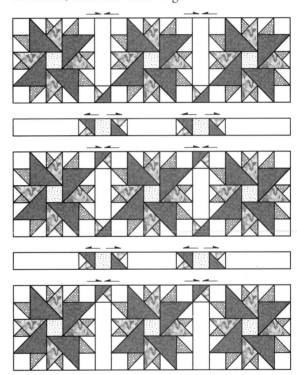

4. Join the rows.

5. Referring to "Plain Borders" on page 57 and the quilt plan on page 49, measure, cut, and add first the light, then the burgundy, purple, and multicolor floral borders.

6. Referring to "Finishing" on pages 57–61, layer the completed quilt top with batting and backing; baste.

7. Quilt as desired, then bind the edges. Label the quilt.

KEY WEST BEAUTY

Color Photo: page 36 ■ **Finished Quilt Size: 43½" x 54½"** ■ **Finished Block Size: 10" x 10"**

Rose print

Green print

Light print

Black print

Multicolor print

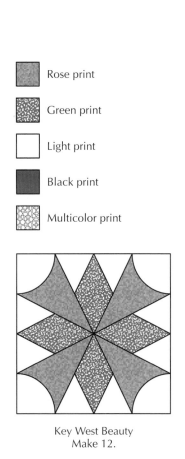

Key West Beauty
Make 12.

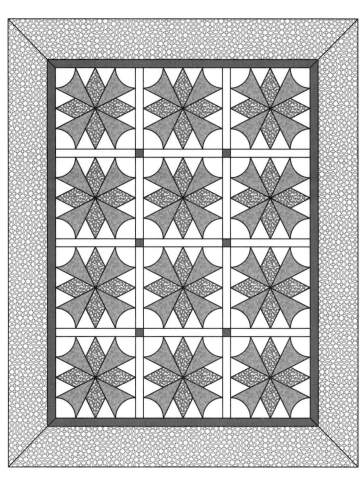

MATERIALS: 42"-WIDE FABRIC

⅞ yd. rose print
½ yd. green print
1⅜ yds. light print
⅜ yd. black print
⅞ yd. multicolor print*
3 yds. for backing
50" x 61" piece of batting
½ yd. for binding

   *If you are using a directional border print, such as the one in the photo, you will need 1⅞ yds. to cut all 4 border strips along the length of the fabric.

CUTTING

   There are no rotary-cutting instructions for this quilt block. Use Templates #12, #13, #14, and #15 on page 64.

From the rose print, cut:
   48 Template #12

From the green print, cut:
   48 Template #13
From the light print, cut:
   48 Template #14
   96 Template #15
   17 strips, each 1½" x 10½", for sashing strips
From the black print, cut:
   4 strips, each 1½" x 40", for inner border
   6 squares, each 1½" x 1½", for cornerstones
From the multicolor print, cut:
   5 strips, each 5" x 40", for outer border (or 4 strips, each 60" long, if cutting lengthwise)
From the binding fabric, cut:
   5 strips, each 2" x 40"

BLOCK ASSEMBLY

Press all seams in direction of arrows unless otherwise instructed.

1. If you have not marked the sewing lines, mark the ¼" intersections on the back of all block pieces. Sew a light triangle (Template #15) to 2 adjacent sides of a green diamond (Template #13).

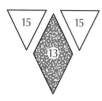

Make 48.

2. Sew a light quarter circle (Template #14) to each pink cone shape (Template #12). Refer to "Curved Seams" on page 28.

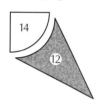

Make 48.

3. Referring to the directions for "Diamonds and Other Central Intersections" on pages 26–27, assemble the Key West block as shown. Make 12 blocks.

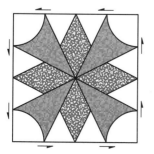

Key West
Make 12.

QUILT TOP ASSEMBLY AND FINISHING

1. Arrange the blocks and sashing strips into 4 rows of 3 blocks each; sew them together in rows. Sew the remaining sashing strips and cornerstones into 3 rows. Press all seams toward the sashing strips.

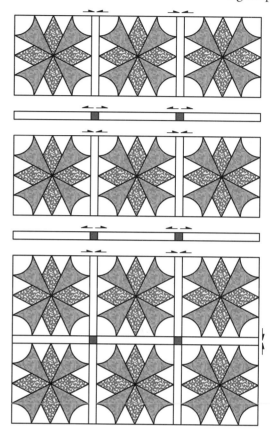

2. Join the rows.
3. Referring to "Mitered Seams" on pages 37–38, measure, cut, and sew the inner and outer borders in place, mitering the corners.
4. Referring to "Finishing" on pages 57–61, layer the completed quilt top with batting and backing; baste.
5. Quilt as desired, then bind the edges. Label the quilt.

MARBLED REFLECTIONS

Color Photo: page 29 ■ **Finished Quilt Size: 51½" x 51½"** ■ **Finished Block Size: 12" x 12"**

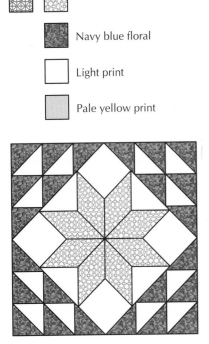

Bright prints

Navy blue floral

Light print

Pale yellow print

Marbled Reflections
Make 9.

MATERIALS: 42"-WIDE FABRIC

⅛ yd. *each* of 9 bright prints for stars
1¾ yds. navy blue floral print
1⅜ yds. light print
½ yd. pale yellow print
3⅜ yds. for backing
58" x 58" piece of batting
½ yd. for binding

TEMPLATE CUTTING

Use Templates #11, #16, #17, and #18 on pages 62–64.
From each of the bright prints, cut:
8 Template #16
From the navy blue floral print, cut:
216 Template #11
From the light print, cut:
108 Template #11
36 Template #17
36 Template #18

ROTARY CUTTING

From each of the bright prints, cut:
1 strip, 2¼" wide. Using a paper template taped to a ruler, crosscut 8 diamonds (Template #16). Refer to "Simple Rotary Cutting" on page 13.
From the navy blue floral print, cut:
2 pieces, each 9" x 39"; cut 9 full bias strips, each 2½" wide, from the pieces. Reserve 2 leftover corner triangles.
54 squares, each 2⅞" x 2⅞"; cut each square once diagonally for 108 half-square triangles
From the light print, cut:
2 pieces, each 9" x 39"; cut 9 full bias strips, each 2½" wide, from the pieces. Reserve 2 leftover corner triangles.
9 squares, each 4⅞" x 4⅞"; cut each square twice diagonally for 36 quarter-square triangles
36 squares, each 3" x 3"

CUTTING FOR BOTH METHODS

From the navy blue floral print, cut:
5 strips, each 4½" x 40", for outer border
From the light print, cut:
4 strips, each 2" x 40", for inner border
From the pale yellow print, cut:
5 strips, each 2½" x 40", for middle border
From the binding fabric, cut:
6 strips, each 2" x 40"

BLOCK ASSEMBLY

Press all seams in direction of arrows unless otherwise instructed.

1. For *template construction*, sew each light triangle (Template #11) to a navy blue triangle (Template #11). Make 108 bias squares. Press 54 squares toward the navy blue and 54 toward the light.

Make 54.   Make 54.

For *rotary construction*, cut the reserved navy blue and light corner triangles into 2½"-wide corner bias strips. Using the navy blue and light full and corner bias strips, make 2 bias-strip units as shown. Press the seams of one strip unit toward the navy blue strips, and the seams of the second strip unit toward the light strips. Cut a total of 108 bias squares, each 2½" x 2½", from the strip units.

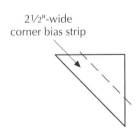

2½"-wide
corner bias strip

2. For either method, arrange the diamonds (Template #16) as shown and sew them into stars, referring to "Diamonds and Other Central Intersections" on pages 26–27.

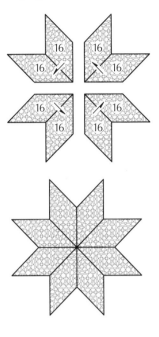

3. Add the light quarter-square triangles (Template #18) and the 3" squares (Template #17) to the stars. See "Set-In Seams" on page 27.

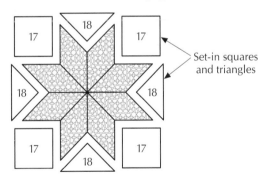

Set-in squares
and triangles

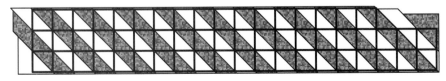

Make 2.
Press 1 to the light, 1 to the dark.

4. Arrange the 108 bias squares and the remaining 108 navy blue half-square triangles (Template #11) as shown and sew them together to assemble the corner units. Pay careful attention to the pressing direction of the bias squares and subsequent seams.

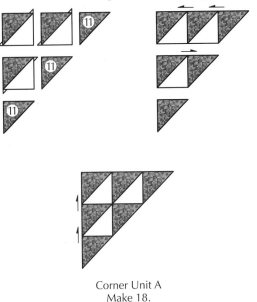

Corner Unit A
Make 18.

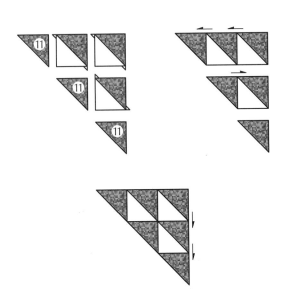

Corner Unit B
Make 18.

5. Sew a corner unit A to 2 opposite sides of each star. Press the seams toward the corner unit. Sew a corner unit B to the remaining 2 sides of each star. Press the seams toward the star. Make 9 blocks.

Corner Unit A
Press toward
corner unit.

Corner Unit B
Press toward star.

Corner Unit B
Press toward star.

Corner Unit A
Press toward
corner unit.

QUILT TOP ASSEMBLY AND FINISHING

1. Arrange the blocks into 3 rows of 3 blocks each. Rotate the blocks so that unit A corners lie next to unit B corners. Diagonal seams should butt. Join the blocks into rows, pressing seams in opposite directions from row to row.

2. Join the rows, pressing seams in either direction.

3. Referring to "Plain Borders" on page 57 and the quilt plan on page 54, measure, cut, and sew first the light, then the pale yellow and navy blue floral borders in place.

4. Referring to "Finishing" on pages 57–61, layer the completed quilt top with batting and backing; baste.

5. Quilt as desired, then bind the edges. Label the quilt.

Finishing

Once your quilt top is pieced, you'll be anxious to finish your quilt. The following information is a brief overview of the basics. The Joy of Quilting series of books from That Patchwork Place address in depth each aspect of quiltmaking. I strongly encourage you to review them for more extensive ideas on machine and hand quilting, setting quilts together, and binding.

ADDING BORDERS

Straighten the edges of the quilt top before adding the borders. There should be little or no trimming needed for a straight-set quilt. A diagonally set quilt is often constructed with oversized side triangles, and you may need to trim these down to size. Align the ¼" line on the ruler with the block points and trim the quilt edges to ¼" from these points. Always position the ¼" line of the ruler along the block points of the adjacent edge at the same time, so the corner will be square when the trimming has been completed.

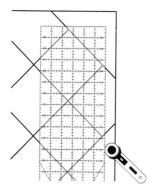

Trim the edges of the quilt
to ¼" from the block points.

PLAIN BORDERS

To find the correct measurement for plain border strips, always measure through the center of the quilt, not at the outside edges. This ensures that the borders on opposite sides of the quilt will be of equal length, and it brings the outer edges into line with the center dimension if discrepancies exist. Otherwise, your quilt might not be "square." Discrepancies are usually the result of minor piecing errors and/or stretching.

1. Sew the border strips together end to end to make one continuous strip. Measure the quilt from the top to the bottom edge through the center of the quilt. From the long strip, cut two border strips to this measurement and pin them to the side edges of the quilt, easing to fit as necessary.

NOTE: If there is a large difference in the two sides or between the center and the sides, it is better to go back and correct the problem now rather than try to make the border fit and end up with a distorted quilt.

2. Sew the side borders in place and press the seams toward the borders.
3. Measure the center width of the quilt, including the side borders, to determine the length of the top and bottom border strips. Cut the borders to this measurement and pin them to the top and bottom edges of the quilt top, again easing to fit as needed. Stitch in place and press the seams toward the border strips.

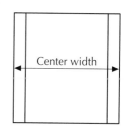

MITERED BORDERS

To make mitered corners, refer to "Mitered Seams" on pages 37–39.

CHOOSING AND MARKING QUILTING DESIGNS

Quilting serves several purposes. The most important is to hold the three layers of the quilt together. Therefore, it is important to do an adequate amount of quilting, whether by hand or machine. The density of the quilting should be consistent so that one area of the quilt does not pucker or bulge as a result of too little or too much quilting. Keep this in mind when choosing your quilt designs; a heavily quilted border will also require heavy quilting in the interior.

There are a tremendous number of sources for quilting designs available commercially. Stencils are immensely popular and readily available. It's a simple matter to trace through the lines to mark the design you want. Some books include drawings of quilt designs that can be transferred in various ways to the quilt top. Simple overall designs, such as cross-hatching, quilting in-the-ditch, outline quilting, and echo quilting are time-honored methods of quilting that do not require commercial stencils or books. Of course, you are free to design your own, too.

Many quilting designs must be marked directly on the quilt top to act as an accurate guide for your stitches. Choose nonpermanent markers for this task—I have seen the beauty of many a quilt ruined by permanent quilt markings. There is a wonderful assortment of wash-out markers available today. With all the time and expense put into the quilt top, it's a comparatively small expense to spend a few dollars on a good marker. Be sure to test a new marker on scrap fabric for washability before using it on your quilt top.

Before marking, press the quilt top one final time. Mark on a hard, flat surface, keeping your marker sharp and your lines clear and fine. It's best to mark the quilt top all at once, but sometimes it is not possible, and you may need to mark as you quilt. If this is the case, do your best to keep the lines from smudging, as you will be marking on a padded surface.

MAKING A QUILT BACKING

The quilt backing, sometimes called the lining, is the back side of the quilt. It must be cut 3" to 4" wider than the quilt top on all sides to allow for any shifting during the quilting process. To determine the size of the quilt backing you need, whether plain or pieced, measure the finished quilt top and add 6" to both length and width. For example, a quilt top that measures 38" x 54" requires a 44" x 60" backing.

The simplest quilt backings to make are plain ones. A plain backing is one piece of fabric without any seams. Many hand quilters prefer this type because there aren't any seams to quilt through. Plain or printed 100% cotton fabrics are available in widths large enough to accommodate all but the largest quilts. Choose a backing width larger than the width of the quilt to allow for shrinkage. To figure how many yards you need, convert the quilt-backing length in inches to yards (divide by 36). Round this figure up to the nearest ⅛ yard and add another ⅛ yard for shrinkage. Purchase this amount.

A paneled backing is similar to a plain backing except that it is pieced in two or three vertical or horizontal panels. The quilt plans in this book contain yardage to make paneled backings, using standard 42"-wide fabric that shrinks to approximately 40". If your quilt backing is more than 40" wide, you need two panels, and a quilt backing more than 80" wide requires three panels.

Figure yardage for vertical panels by doubling or tripling the quilt-backing length in inches, depending on the number of panels needed. Divide this figure by 36, round up to the nearest ⅛ yard, and add another ⅛ yard for shrinkage.

Use crosswise-pieced panels when your quilt's length is less than 74". Figure yardage for crosswise panels by doubling the quilt-backing width in inches. Divide this figure by 36, round up to the nearest ⅛ yard, and add ⅛ yard more for shrinkage.

Two ways to piece paneled backings

Crosswise panel

An increasingly popular and fun way to make a quilt backing is to piece one from many different fabrics. It can be pieced from large squares, triangles, rectangles, and "mistakes" left over from the quilt top or even other coordinating prints that you have on hand. No matter what you do, a pieced backing is considerably less expensive, uses leftovers, and is totally delightful to discover on the back of a quilt. See an example of a pieced backing in the "Gallery" on page 33.

BASTING THE QUILT LAYERS

The quilt sandwich is composed of the quilt top, backing, and a filler material called *batting*. There are many battings available in both synthetic and natural fibers. Entire books are devoted to the advantages and disadvantages of the different types. Whatever batting you choose, be sure to read and follow the manufacturer's instructions for any preparation that may be required. The batting should be the same size as your backing. I open packaged batting and lay it flat and covered (I have cats!) on a bed overnight to relax the wrinkles and creases.

Once the quilting designs are marked, the backing made, and a batting bought and prepared, you are ready to secure the three layers with basting. Press the backing smooth, then tape it, right side down, to a hard, clean, flat work surface, such as a table or floor. Do not use a surface that you don't want marred with pin marks! Securely tape the sides of the backing every few inches. Tape the corners last, being careful not to stretch the bias. Center the batting over the backing and smooth it in place. Carefully place the quilt top over the batting right side up. Smooth it and begin pin basting it to the other layers, always working from the center out. This will work out any unevenness in the layers.

For hand quilting, use a light-colored thread to baste the sandwich in a 3" to 4" grid, again working from the center out. Baste across both diagonals of the sandwich to stabilize the bias. Finish by securing the edges of the quilt sandwich with a line of stitches around the edge. Remove the pins.

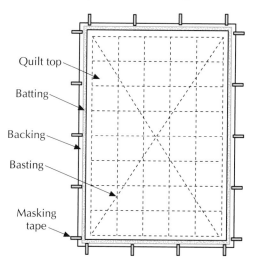

Quilt top
Batting
Backing
Basting
Masking tape

Many machine quilters and even some hand quilters prefer to use special quilter's safety pins rather than thread to baste the sandwich. Recently, some quilters have begun to use plastic tacks, such as those used to secure price tags to clothing. They are available at quilt and hobby shops or through mail-order catalogs.

QUILTING

I have no expertise in machine quilting and recommend you refer to books by experts in that field for how-to information. *Machine Quilting Made Easy* by Maurine Noble (That Patchwork Place) is a good resource. I do hand quilt, though, and will briefly review the basics.

Quilting is a simple running stitch that goes through all three layers of the quilt sandwich. All quilting should be done from the center out. Most quilters prefer to use some type of frame to hold the three layers together to prevent them from shifting during quilting.

Quilting needles are called Betweens and come in different sizes. The larger the number, the smaller the needle and the smaller your stitches. Try to use the smallest needle you can comfortably handle. The eyes are tiny, so many people use a needle threader to thread them. Use cotton hand-quilting thread cut into 12" to 18" lengths. Longer threads will weaken from sliding through the eye continuously. I strongly recommend that you use a thimble on your stitching finger. Some quilters also use one on the "receiving" finger (the finger under the quilt).

1. Begin quilting with a small, single knot tied close to the end of the thread. Slip the needle between the layers of the quilt about a needle length's distance from your chosen starting point. If possible, weave the needle through a seam allowance. Bring the needle up where you want to start and give the thread a tug to lodge the knot in the batting or seam.

2. Following the quilting marks, sew a simple running stitch, being sure to catch all three layers with each stitch. Ideally, the stitches on the back of the quilt should be the same size as the stitches on the front. All stitches should be of consistent size and evenly spaced. This can take some practice. It is better to sacrifice small stitch size in favor of even spacing and consistent size.

3. End a line of quilting by forming a small knot in the thread about ⅛" from where it exits the quilt. Take the last stitch between the layers only and run the needle a short distance away from the last stitch before bringing the needle up, out of the quilt. Again, weaving the thread in and out of a seam allowance before exiting will strengthen the quilting. Give a gentle tug, and the knot will slip between the layers. Clip the thread a short distance from the quilt top and let the tail slip back between the layers.

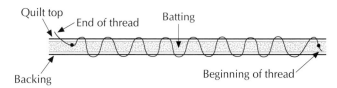

4. Continue to quilt, working from the center of the quilt toward the edges to ease out any fullness. Finish all the quilting and remove the interior basting stitches before binding the quilt. Leave the perimeter basting stitches in place to hold the edges for the binding.

ADDING A SLEEVE

If you plan to display your finished quilt on the wall, you will need to add a hanging sleeve, and it's best to add it before you bind the quilt.

1. Using leftover fabric or a piece of muslin, cut a strip 6" to 8" wide and 1" shorter than the width of the quilt at the top edge. Fold the ends under ½", then ½" again, and stitch.

2. Fold the fabric strip in half lengthwise, wrong sides together, and baste the raw edges to the top edge of the quilt back. The top edge of the sleeve will be secured when the binding is sewn onto the quilt.

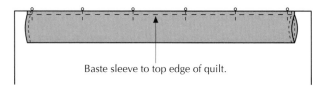

Baste sleeve to top edge of quilt.

3. Finish the sleeve after the binding has been attached by blindstitching the bottom of the sleeve in place. Push the bottom edge of the sleeve up just a bit to provide a little give so the hanging rod does not put strain on the quilt itself.

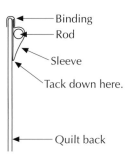

Binding
Rod
Sleeve
Tack down here.
Quilt back

BINDING THE QUILT

The binding fabric requirements for the quilt plans in this book are based on cutting straight-of-grain fabric strips for a double-fold binding. This is a simple, but durable, binding.

To make the binding:

1. Cut 2"-wide strips from selvage to selvage for a standard ¼"-wide finished binding.

2. Join the strips at right angles and stitch across the corner. Make one long piece of binding. Trim excess fabric and press the seams open. It is important to use closely matching threads in this situation to avoid peekaboo stitches at the seams.

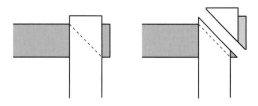

3. Fold the strip in half lengthwise, wrong sides together, and press. Trim one end of the strip at a 45° angle, then turn under ¼" and press.

Fold line

To attach the binding:

1. Baste the three layers of the quilt securely at the outer edges if you have not already done so.
2. Trim the batting and backing even with the quilt-top edges. Square the corners if necessary.
3. In the center of one edge of the quilt, align the raw edges of the binding with the raw edges of the quilt top. Leaving about 6" free as a starting tail, sew the binding to the edge of the quilt with a ¼"-wide seam allowance. Stop stitching ¼" from the corner of the first side. (It's a good idea to pin-mark ¼" in from the corner before you begin sewing.) Backstitch and remove the quilt from the machine.

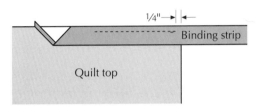

4. To create a neat, mitered turn at the corner, flip the binding straight up from the corner so that it forms a continuous line with the adjacent side of the quilt top.

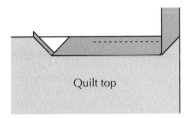

5. Fold the binding straight down so it lies on top of the adjacent side, being careful not to shift the pleat formed at the fold. Pin the pleat in place. Pin-mark ¼" in from the next corner. Starting at the edge, stitch the second side of the binding to the quilt, stopping at the ¼" mark. Repeat the same process for the remaining corners.

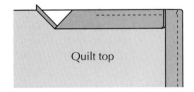

6. When you reach the beginning of the binding, overlap the binding tails by about 1" and cut away any excess; trim the end at a 45° angle. Tuck the end of the binding into the fold and finish the seam.

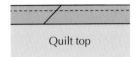

7. Turn the binding to the back of the quilt. Slipstitch the fold of the binding to the quilt backing. Slipstitch the miters in place on both front and back to complete the binding—and your quilt!

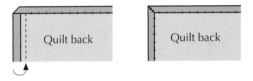

LABELING YOUR QUILT

Be sure to sign and date your quilt. Labels can be elaborate or simple, and can be handwritten, typed, or embroidered. Be sure to include the name of the quilt, your name, your city and state, the date, and the name of the recipient if it is a gift. Add any other interesting or important information about the quilt. Future generations will want to know more about the quilt than just who made it and when.

Templates

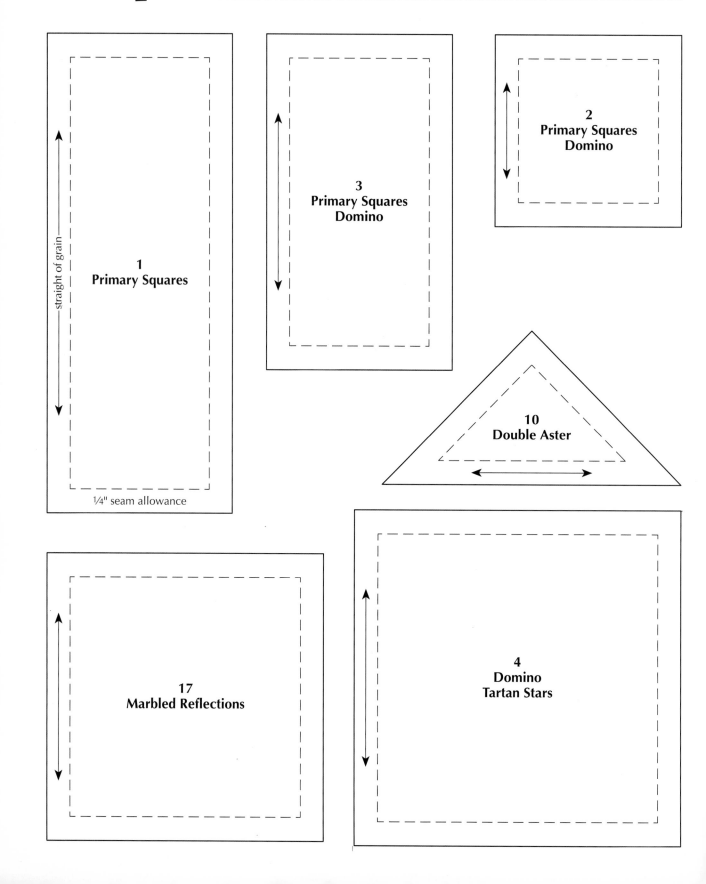

**1
Primary Squares**

straight of grain

¼" seam allowance

**3
Primary Squares
Domino**

**2
Primary Squares
Domino**

**10
Double Aster**

**17
Marbled Reflections**

**4
Domino
Tartan Stars**

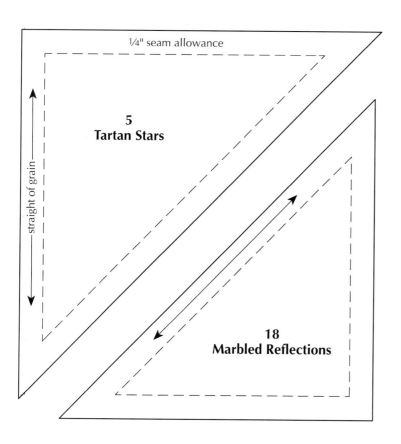

1/4" seam allowance

5
Tartan Stars

straight of grain

18
Marbled Reflections

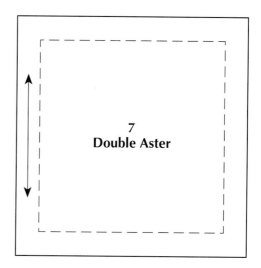

7
Double Aster

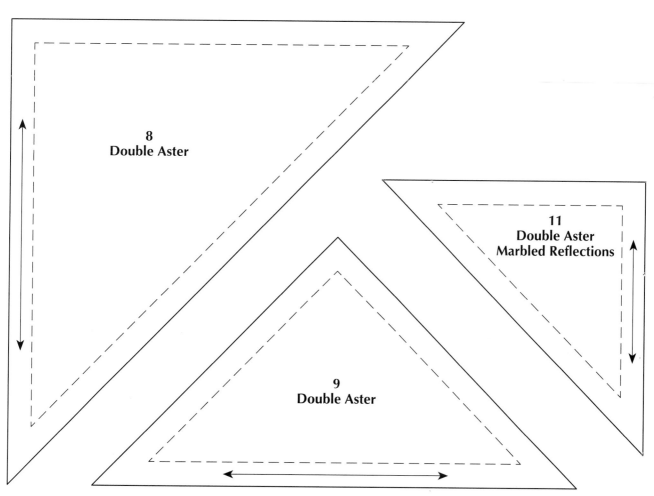

8
Double Aster

11
Double Aster
Marbled Reflections

9
Double Aster

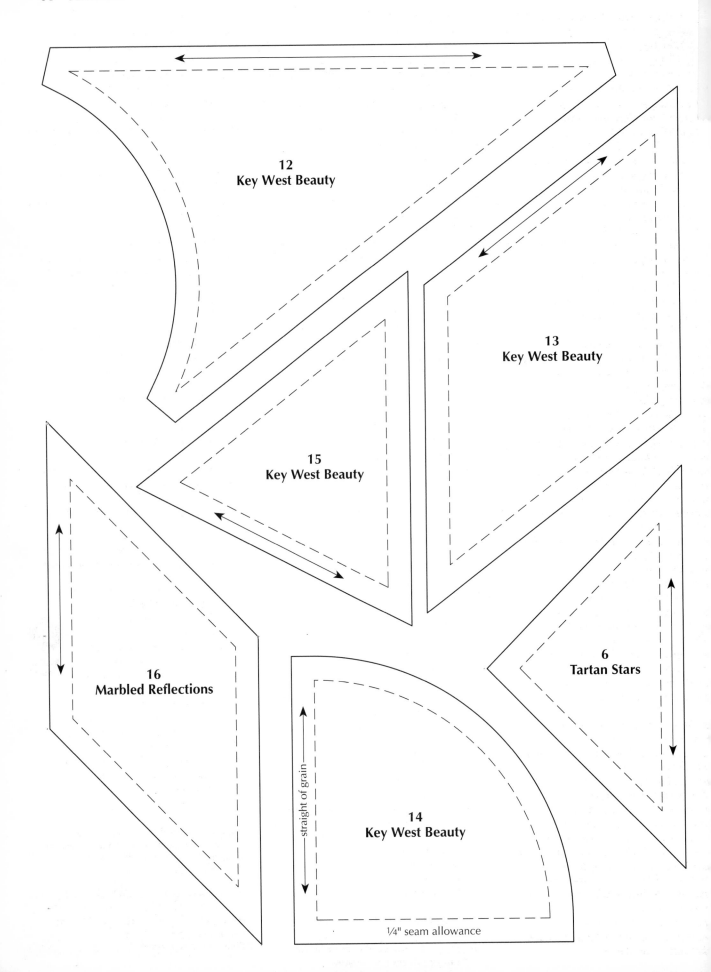

12
Key West Beauty

13
Key West Beauty

15
Key West Beauty

16
Marbled Reflections

6
Tartan Stars

straight of grain

14
Key West Beauty

¼" seam allowance